Millionaire Real Estate Agent Makeover

First Impressions Are Your Paycheck

To my Mom and Dad

(Look Ma, I really did it!!!)

Copyright © 2014 by Aisha Jones

All rights reserved. No part of this publication may be reproduced, distributed, or transmitted in any form or by any means, including photocopying, recording, or other electronic or mechanical methods, without the prior written permission of the publisher, except in the case of brief quotations embodied in critical reviews and certain other noncommercial uses permitted by copyright law. For permission requests, write to the publisher, addressed "Attention: Permissions Coordinator," at the address below.

Contents

CHAPTER 1
The Stylish Realtor — 13

CHAPTER 2
The Maintained Realtor — 29

CHAPTER 3
The Shapely Realtor — 46

CHAPTER 4
The Vibrant Realtor — 61

CHAPTER 5
The Gilded Realtor — 82

CHAPTER 6
The Powerful Realtor — 101

CHAPTER 7
The Photogenic Realtor — 116

CHAPTER 8
The Confident Realtor — 132

CHAPTER 9
The Gracious Realtor — 148

CHAPTER 10
The Millionaire Realtor — 164

Appendix A:
101 Accessories List — 180

Appendix B:
7 Deadly Sins of a Head Shot Photo — 184

Appendix C:
Answers to Chapter 4's Fill-in the Blanks — 186

Appendix D:
Your Color Season — 187

Appendix E:
Emergency Checklist — 188

Appendix F:
Style Net Worth Quiz — 189

Appendix G:
The "Just One Thing" Plan — 194

Introduction

"Caveat emptor"

"Caveat emptor" means "let the buyer beware" in Latin. That is probably an unusual way to start off a book you just picked up (thank you for that, by the way). I started the book this way because I want you to dive into this book with your eyes wide open like Zooey Deschenal in—well, anything. (The girl is gorgeous, but she does have really big eyes, which of course make her more gorgeous.)

I want your eyes wide open and wanting to take some action. If you bought this book thinking it would be just like a fuller Cosmo magazine with fashion and beauty advice, then this isn't the book for you. (I did try to work in some advice on orgasms and sex positions, but I couldn't justify discussing that when talking about open houses - so it made the cutting room floor.)

If you bought this book thinking it would make you a slick salesperson and teach you the single phrase necessary to get clients to close or how to lull your clients into a lucid hypnotic state with the latest sales gimmick, then this is also not the book for you. (I admit it would be cool to have that superpower, but it brings up ethical concerns—like do you make them strip naked and walk across the street just so you an your friends can have a laugh.)

So who is this book for? This is a book for anyone who laughed at those previous jokes, because we would get along famously. But really, this is for the woman that is a realtor, who knows that there must be a better way to do things. This for the woman who has ever looked at another professional woman and thought, "How does she always look so perfectly put together?" This is for the woman who knows her true potential in the competitive real estate field, but just can't quite seem to connect the last few dots. This book walks you through those last few dots. It gives you the last puzzle pieces that complete the picture.

In this book, you will find beauty and fashion advice. You won't find trends. You'll find timeless fashion advice so you can look fashionable in your clothes for a long time and get more bang for your buck. The beauty advice is not some long regiment that you have to go through every morning, afternoon, and evening. It is advice that works for your on-the-go lifestyle, so no matter where you are, you can look fabulous even when you are driving over to a property with clients.

Here is the part of the book that will surprise you. You are going to find solid business and marketing ideas to elevate your image so you can get more and better clients who give you more and better referrals. It creates the cycle of success. You look better, so you get better clients, so you make more money, so you look even better and get even better clients, and so on and so on—an endless cycle of success.

Throughout the book, you'll see sections where you can get more in-depth "reader only" access on the website www.MillionaireRealEstateAgentMakeover.com

At the end of each chapter, there is an end of chapter bonus that gives very specific business actions you can take to move yourself and your business forward.

Here are some of the highlights about what is contained in this book:

- ◊ Everything you need to know about how the Top 250 realtors in the country dress.
- ◊ The guilt-free way to never overlook a client by establishing this specific policy in your business.
- ◊ 4 surprising games you can play to boost your confidence.

- 6 secrets to dressing slimmer - no detoxing required.
- The best way to radiate "power" with a single outfit.
- Looking better = More confidence = ???
- Your color and branding blueprint to stand out in the marketplace.
- 20 questions you should ask to make sure you have a killer professional head shot.
- Cashmere! Diamonds! Pearls! You are about to be very happy (and so is your wallet).
- A tale of two types of realtors - One is a group with the highest sales volume, the other...
- How to "WOW" the neighbors and generate referrals.
- Your beauty repair kit - goodbye uni-brow and yellow teeth.
- Calling all women with less than perfect bodies. Discover tricks to flatter your figure and skyrocket your confidence.
- The 21 day challenge to stimulate referrals.
- Are you too nice for your own good? A practice to start standing up for yourself.
- And much, much, more...

This book truly is a labor of love, and I hope each of you sits down in front of a fireplace with a warm cup of hot chocolate with marshmallows shaped like hearts to devour this book like a warm scone on a crisp morning. Wait, I'm not Martha Stewart. Disregard that last sentence. This book was time-consuming because it contains so much information. I don't care if you read it in front of the fireplace or holding it one-handed while breast feeding – just read it!

I want you to read it because it can help you make more money and change your life and the lives of your children (and potentially the lives of your jewelers—why should rappers be the only ones that can buy "bling" once they've made it?)

Remember the formula:

Look Better = More Confidence = More Clients = More Money

Happy reading!!

P.S. If you were less than a stellar student in school, there is the Just Do One Thing Plan located in Appendix G. It's like peeking over the shoulder of Poindexter who has all the answers in class (FYI, I was Poindexter in my classes - I joke to hide the pain!)

CHAPTER 1

The Stylish Realtor

You Hate This Woman

You hate this woman! You know who I am talking about. She has flawless makeup, not a hair out of place, and her wardrobe seems to have come off a Hollywood set. She has kids, is great at her job, and looks contented as if she spent the prior evening having multiple orgasms with her husband who could easily step in for Brad Pitt if he ever became ill and could not complete a movie.

You hate this woman because she appears to be the exception to the saying, "You can't have it all." You hate this woman because ultimately she makes you feel like less of woman, like you are a complete and utter failure. Not because there is always a rogue hair that escapes from your ponytail or that your pants bear a tell-tale pumpkin spice latte stain. You feel like a failure because you wish you had her confidence, encased in such a pretty, well put together package.

This woman may be your neighbor, your co-worker, or even your sister-in-law. But she is most likely staring back at you from a magazine cover in line at the grocery store while you guilt trip yourself about the peanut M&M's you just placed in your basket. She is smiling at you from the cover. The sub-headlines talk about the organic cookbook she just wrote, her 2-hour exercise routine, and the nonprofit she started in Africa.

As you tear into the bag of M&M's (because who can wait a whole 45 seconds for checkout), you placate yourself by saying, "I could look that good if I had a team of people working for me. In real life, she is probably cross-eyed and has bad skin." And you chuckle to yourself as you exit the grocery store.

You may be laughing, but the joke is on you. That "perfect woman" knows something that you don't, and she is laughing all the way to the bank…

The Joke Is On You

The "perfect woman" on the magazine cover knows that her first impression and appearance directly affect her bank account. She knows that if she looks great on a red carpet, in a TV appearance, or in unexpected Paparazzi shots, there will be directors, producers, and writers watching who may call her agent and book her for a job. It is in her best interest to look great if she wants to continue to live a fabulous life, have a cushy retirement, and put her kids through college. Therefore, it is worth her time, energy, and money to make sure she looks great. There is a significant ROI to being well put together.

Are you still laughing?

Believe it or not, as a real estate professional you have a lot in common with the magazine cover model. There is significant ROI in being well put together. Research shows that the top real estate agents in the country invest in their appearance and out earn many of their contemporaries. Maybe you can take a lesson from them and decide to get your act together. After all, don't you want to live a fabulous life, have a cushy retirement, and put your kids through college?

You don't have to do this alone—you have this book, and you may even acquire a part-time team to help you get the job done. But before we get started, we must agree on a very important point...

You Can Meet A New Client Anywhere

We've all done this. We had a day where things were extra hectic or we were sick, so we decided to just go to the store looking less than our best. We may have even been in the store in pajamas and wearing flip-flops so old that you are sure they used to belong to Moses. You are at the store trying to just run in and get out as fast as possible, and you run into an ex-boyfriend, your old boss, or the best looking man in the world. Every time that happens, you have just been introduced to Murphy's Law, "Whatever can go wrong, will go wrong." Since your clients are your business, and clients equal referrals, isn't it in your best interest to stay on the right side of Murphy's Law?

The line at Starbucks, your kid's soccer games, and the mall are great places to meet people, i.e. potential clients. Looking your best at all times will help you to look professional and detail-oriented when you hand over your business card to your new friend. There is also a hidden benefit...

It's All About Confidence

What if you had a fairy godmother? What if one day she gave you a small vial containing a light pink elixir? She then tells you that the magic elixir is confidence, and if you just put a few drops on your tongue it will give you the confidence of Donald Trump (but without any of the arrogance or bad hair). When would you use the elixir? During job interviews, first dates, important client meetings. Well, there is a magic elixir and it involves being well-dressed and well-groomed. You feel great and a confident energy just emanates from you and attracts others.

Your wardrobe makeover will trigger an influx of confidence that you may have previously thought could only come from a fairy godmother. Not only will your professional appearance attract more clients, but it will make you more confident when you open your mouth to speak to them. It is the double whammy—beauty and smarts. Now others will want to bottle you and make their own elixir.

If you had more confidence, what would your career look like? What kind of clients would you have? How many office sales records could you break? What publications would you be featured in? This better version of you could create your dream career and your dream lifestyle.

The best part of this is that it is a never ending cycle. You dress better, so you get more confidence. Your increased confidence allows you to get more and better clients and start making money. With that additional money, you start dressing even better and gain even more confidence because you are more successful and you start getting more clients and making even more money. Don't you see the cycle just continues? It is like starting off with a standby plane ticket and then getting upgraded to coach and then upgraded to first class and then upgraded to business class where you meet Madonna and she wants you to sell a house for her.

The success formula is:

WARDROBE = CONFIDENCE = MORE CLIENTS = MILLIONAIRE SUCCESS.

How To Get Started?

Before you start designing your private plane, we need to first cover some basics. If forty pages into this book I anger you and you want to throw this book into the nearest trash receptacle, please tear this chapter out of the book and throw out the rest. This section is that important. (And if you throw out the book, please bury it under the other trash because according to Murphy's Law, my mother will walk past that trash bin and be ever so disappointed.)

If you just do what is discussed in this chapter, you will be light years ahead of your colleagues and well on your way to receiving the "Best Dressed in the Office" award with minimal effort on your part. Even Bernie Madoff could not offer that kind of return on your investment.

There are twelve essential pieces needed in your wardrobe. These are the foundational pieces that make a wardrobe. I refer to them as the 12 Apostles of Style. You may already have some of these items in your wardrobe. If you do not, then you need to get busy acquiring them. These are going to make it easy to mix and match, and if you do not have the time or money to complete the other wardrobe makeover steps, then you can still pull off a minimally chic look with these items until you jump income brackets.

The 12 Apostles Of Style - Real Estate Edition

Why do I call them apostles? I call them apostles because "apostle" simply means "messenger." These items are the foundation, and they communicate to everyone that you are stylish, professional, and confident. Here are the 12 items that are going to help you send a message to your industry:

1. ____ Ballet flats
2. ____ Men's white shirt
3. ____ Cashmere turtleneck or sweater
4. ____ Trench coat
5. ____ Little black dress
6. ____ Classic black high heels
7. ____ Diamond earrings
8. ____ Suit
9. ____ Jeans

10. ____ Pearl necklace
11. ____ Pencil skirt
12. ____ Cardigan

The 1st Apostle - The Ballet Flat

The ballet flat allows you to be stylish and still keep your podiatrist happy. As a real estate agent, you can have really long days running around to different properties and hosting open houses. The ballet flat will allow you to be stylish even if you have to be on your feet all day. It is also a great option for those women who do not know how to wear heels. (I've realized that these women do exist; previously, I thought it was a myth like a white unicorn).

Where to wear: These shoes can work great if you have an important meeting or event. They should also be the default shoe for the weekends as you interact with potential clients in more casual settings—for example, your kid's softball game.

Wear with what: These shoes can be worn with suits, dress, skirts, jeans, and even shorts. That is why these shoes are the first apostle—versatility.

The 2nd Apostle - Men's White Shirt

You may already own this shirt or own a close cousin of this shirt. This shirt should have buttons down the front, cuffs, be extremely white, and extra crisp. This shirt can go with almost anything and is an easy option to go with any suit.

Where to wear: This shirt can be worn to any event under the sun…no really, you can wear it open and tied in the front to a pool party. It is simple and classic and will go with every suit, skirt, and pair of pants that you own.

Wear with what: This is the perfect shirt to wear with suits or even under a short sleeved or sleeveless dress. It can also be paired with jeans for a classic and clean look.

The 3rd Apostle - Cashmere Turtleneck or Sweater

This sweater is a classic and you will have it for years and years. It is a way to instantly look pulled together and polished. Even if you live in a climate with warmer weather, this item is a must have. I recommend black, chocolate brown, gray, navy, or ivory for maximum versatility. If I were starting from scratch, I would choose black.

Where to wear: This sweater can be worn to almost any of your professional events since it can go with a suit. It is also a great item to look pulled together on the weekend with a pair of jeans or stylish khaki's.

Wear with what: This sweater goes great with a pencil skirt, suit, or even a pair of jeans. With a non-turtleneck sweater, you can even wear it with your men's white shirt by pulling the shirt collar so it is on the outside of the neckline of the sweater.

How to Buy Cashmere

Number three on the Apostles of Style list is a cashmere sweater or cardigan. If you haven't bought cashmere before, don't be scared. Even though it has the word "cash" in its name, buying cashmere does not require a black American Express card. The trick to buying cashmere is to get the best quality at the lowest price. I just have to train you in what to look for so you can spot quality.

Tip #1: The easiest way is to look at the label. It will state what percentage of the garment is cashmere. This is fairly intuitive. 100% cashmere is going to be higher quality than 10% cashmere.

Tip #2: This tip is going to require you to do some profiling. The best cashmere is going to come from two places: Scotland and Italy. Again look at the label to see in which country the garment was made.

Tip #3: Test the garments resilience. You might need to turn your back to the salesgirl in order to do this, but you are going to want to grab the sides of the sweater and pull. If the sweater springs back to its original shape, then it is good quality. If not, you are going to want to hide that sweater at the bottom of the pile and get the hell out of there before they force you to buy it because you ruined the shape of the sweater.

The 4th Apostle - Trench Coat

You need something chic to wear over your chic outfits, and the trench coat will do the trick. It is something you can wear over your most dressed up outfit, and looks extra sexy with classic black high heels.

Where to wear: Throw this on over your outfit when it is extra blustery outside, or to dress up a more casual outfit. Looks great draped over a chair or couch at business meetings. You also look super hero-esque with it flowing behind you as you enter a building.

Wear with what: Wear this over your suits or dress up jeans and ballet flats with this trench coat.

The 5th Apostle - The Little Black Dress

A wardrobe piece so nice that you have to put a "The" in front of it. This is the default option for an event where you have to be dressed up. This dress goes with a classic style such as a sheath dress (Google the image of the dress in Michelle Obama's first portrait as First Lady).

Where to wear: Wear this dress when you need to be a little dressed up. This can also be worn in other professional settings if paired with a jacket.

Wear with what: This dress can go with your ballet flats or classic black high heels. You can also switch it up by wearing your cashmere sweater or men's white shirt under the dress depending on the neckline of the LBD. The best part of this dress is that you can accessorize it a million different ways and no one will know that it is the same dress.

The 6th Apostle - Classic Black High Heels

Do these even need any explanation? We all know what these are. However, here is a fashion tip: go with a pointed option, as it will lengthen your leg and give you a more slimming look.

Where to wear: Wear these shoes to any professional setting or any professional events.

Wear with what: These shoes should go with any of your professional outfits, including your little black dress.

The 7th Apostle - Diamond Earrings

Of course there had to be some bling in the list of the twelve apostles. These earrings are versatile and can be dressed up or dressed down. In fact I love them a little bit more if they are worn with jeans and a t-shirt. If you can't afford the real thing, fake it—a little cubic zirconia never hurt anybody.

Where to wear: Absolutely everywhere, darling!

Wear with what: Absolutely everything, darling!

The 8th Apostle - Suit

Suit up. This is essentially the uniform for professionals so it absolutely had to be included in this list. Another fashion tip: if you are buying a suit, buy the pants, jacket, and matching skirt all at the same time. It will give you infinitely more perfectly matched mix-and-match options. (Make sure to read Chapter 6.)

Where to wear: Wear this when you need to look like a total pro. This is great for first-time meetings with clients, prospecting for new clients, or attending events.

Wear with what: This suit is great to wear with your men's white shirt or with a cashmere sweater. It will also work great with either your ballet flats or your black classic high heels.

The 9th Apostle - Jeans

The uniform of Americans. The secret is to have a great fitting pair of jeans. Yes you might even need to try on 20 pair of jeans to get it just right. Just think of yourself as the Goldilocks of jeans.

Where to wear: Although not appropriate in all professional settings, there are ways to dress up in jeans. Depending on your clientele, jeans may sometimes be called for. However, jeans are always a great option for the weekends because you never know who you are going to bump into.

Wear with what: Try wearing a pair of jeans with your men's white shirt, suit jacket, and ballet flats.

The 10th Apostle - Pearl Necklace

If you could only have one necklace in your closet, this should be your choice because it goes with so many things, including your diamond earrings. However, you do not have to get your grandma's pearl necklace. They now have many varieties including multi-strand necklaces. As usual, if you can't afford the real thing, get as close to the real thing as possible. Don't think of yourself as frugal—think of yourself as pro-Oyster.

Where to wear: Wear when you need to look professional, classic, and detail oriented.

Wear with what: Goes great with your little black dress, men's white shirt, and adds a feminine touch to masculine suits.

The 11th Apostle - Pencil Skirt

This is possibly one of the most universally figure-flattering skirt styles. The pencil skirt helps you to look pulled together and sleek. For an extra slimming effect get with a length that ends right below the knee, but right before your calf juts out.

Where to wear: Wear this anyplace you would wear a suit. The pencil skirt allows you to be a little more feminine.

Wear with what: Men's white shirt, cashmere sweater. It goes with almost anything. You can wear it with a t-shirt and denim jacket for a weekend look or casual Friday.

The 12th Apostle - Cardigan

A great alternative to the suit jacket. The cardigan allows you to have a professional but softer look. Any outfit you wear with your suit, you can also wear with a great cardigan. It is also a quick option to quickly pull an outfit together on the weekend.

Where to wear: Dress it up or dress it down, that is the magic of the cardigan. You can wear this in your many professional environments or during your personal "off the clock" time.

Wear with what: Wear this with your suit pants, men's white shirt and a great belt worn around the cardigan.

Put Pants On One Leg At A Time

We all put our pants on one leg at a time. It takes just as much time to put on a pair of suit pants as it does to put on a pair of jeans. You can no longer use the excuse that you do not have the time to dress nice. In fact, it may take longer to put on the jeans because there is usually a lot more bending and stretching that needs to occur (skinny jeans, thou art my nemesis and I vow to one day to avenge my newly fragile self esteem.)

What Is The Secret Of Glamour?

When Oscar De La Renta was asked the question, "What is the secret to glamour?", he gave a one word answer:

DISCIPLINE

We hate the word discipline. It means that we have to turn down the cheesecake dessert or put on running shoes at 6 a.m. when your bed is warm and cozy (and hopefully contains a gorgeous man). Discipline is not fun, but discipline can have amazing results.

This makeover takes discipline. Changing your life always takes discipline, just ask any former drug addict. This makeover takes discipline because it requires you to make different choices on a daily basis. You have to choose the jeans over sweats, and choose flats over sneakers (most of the time). I am acknowledging that for some of you, this change will not be easy. It will be hard to be motivated every day.

To help you stay motivated, you can connect with me on Facebook, Twitter, Google Plus, and receive makeover motivation on a regular basis. See the resources section in the appendix for more information.

There is another fun game you can play to stay motivated.

Pretend you are being hounded by the paparazzi.

If you were a starlet that was constantly being hounded by the paparazzi, you would have to be careful of how you looked because that photo could end up on the cover of a magazine that is stocked in every grocery store checkout lane. Before you step out of the house, think—would I want to see this on the cover of a magazine? If the answer is no, go back inside, tidy up a bit and emerge from the house more stylish and more put together.

Make sure that whenever you go outside of the house, you are always paparazzi-ready. This includes leaving the house to work out. Working out is a great time to meet new people and network. (This is tough for me. I look like a homeless person when I am working out. Homeless Booty Boot Camp coming to a DVD player near you!)

What Was She Thinking?

During the real estate boom of the 2000's, my mother-in-law (like many other people) decided to go into the real estate business. She studied and got her real estate license and became an agent at one of the major real estate firms.

One day she came in triumphantly before dinner and proclaimed that she just came back from showing a property. It was a large ranch style house that included a significant amount of surrounding land. From her description of the property, one could easily tell that this gentleman had to be well off to be able afford this property. However, I was stunned. I was not stunned by the gorgeous property description and large price tag, but I was stunned because of what she was wearing. She did not in any way represent herself as a successful professional. She was wearing an extremely frumpy outfit that I had seen her wear many a Sunday afternoon; to see clients in this outfit was close to blasphemy. I couldn't imagine someone doing something so careless with their career and not at least showing respect to a client by putting some visible effort into their appearance when meeting them.

Needless to say, my mother-in-law did not get the client and she didn't sell the property. Her career in real estate was fairly short-lived.

It really would not have taken much for her to look more put together. There is a reason that this is the subject matter of Chapter 1. It is the foundation of everything. As you can see, it does not take a lot of time and money to acquire these items. You could set a goal of acquiring one item a month and by the end of the year, you will have these foundational pieces and already be dressing better.

I equate this to baking a cake. You need the basic ingredients of flour, sugar, milk, and 6butter. A real estate professional's wardrobe requires the twelve foundational pieces described above. That is what you need to be a properly baked cake. Right now, you don't even have enough to look like dessert. You are being mistaken for goulash, or a stew, or sprig of parsley that people brush off the plate. We need to get you looking like something people look forward to. You are the icing on top of their real estate concerns. You make it easier to digest.

Now, it would be boring just having a plain old pound cake day after day. If you add red food coloring, it can be a Red Velvet Cake and stand out on the shelf. Or a little bit of lemon makes it into a lemon cake that makes people salivate. Think of these small changes as the slight adjustments to your wardrobe; these are the things that make your brand. These are also the things that people hire wardrobe stylists for. They can bake a regular cake, but they need a cake that is going to stand out from all the other cakes. It really does not take much to make these wardrobe variations. At the end of the book, I provide many of these resources to help you out in this mixing and matching process.

End-Of-Chapter Bonu$:

Make some extra deposits in your style and business bank account with this tip:

your business card is a basic accessory

We have talked about business basics, but what about basics for your business? Your business card is an essential business accessory. In fact, it could be the thirteenth Apostle of Style. Your business card also communicates volumes about you.

You never know where you are going to run into a great business opportunity, so you need to be prepared at all times. Your business cards need to be with you. Your business cards reflect your personality and your branding. With many real estate companies, they have standard cards that they issue to realtors. See if it is possible to deviate from this and get your own cards so that they will stand out.

So here is the tip: You are going to give a great free offer to everyone you give your card to. In order to do this, your cards need to meet these two requirements:

You need to have cards that you can write on

Your cards need to be designed so that there is an area that you can write on

Here's how your networking conversation will go:

Potential Client or Referral Source: So you are in real estate?

You: Yes. I'm a realtor. Here let me give you my card. Let me write this on here. If you give this code to anyone at my office, they will know that you are a VIP and you can get a free comparison and pricing analysis on your home.

As you are giving them the sales pitch, you are writing down a special phrase or code on the card such as "LISA VIP." Do you think this person is more likely to hold onto your card? Of course they are. You made them feel special. Everyone likes to feel like a VIP and you have personalized the card.

The impact of this networking strategy is increased twofold if you have amazing and stylish business cards that match your overall branding. It communicates that you, too, are a Very Important

Person, and that attracts people. Additionally, a nicer card indicates something of value and it is harder for people to throw away.

There is an additional marketing benefit. You now have an effective way to track your networking effectiveness. You can keep track of how many people called in and used the phrase "LISA VIP." You know that these people came to you as a result of your business cards. How is that for tracking ROI?

There will be more on business accessories, branding, and business colors in subsequent chapters. In the meantime, start carrying around this must-have accessory for the millionaire real estate agent...the business card.

CHAPTER 2

The Maintained Realtor

Geez, you sure are nifty! If we were in a malt shop and sporting a poodle skirt, then a guy calling us "nifty" would be the bees knees (wait, I think I am mixing decades). Either way, if chapter 1 was the most important chapter, then chapter 2 is the second most important chapter. In order to implement chapter 2, we must remember to be nifty or, more accurately, we must remember to be NEFT-Y. But we will get there shortly. First things first...

So you completed chapter 1. You are dressing better. Your friends, family and colleagues are noticing. You may have noticed that your prospects and clients are responding better. You may even have observed that your back is a little straighter, your chin is held a little higher, and there is more of a switch in your hips. Those physical symptoms are called increased confidence. Let's kick that confidence into the stratosphere by addressing another important issue not necessarily associated with your wardrobe, but it has to do with style maintenance. The important lesson of this chapter is style maintenance, or a simple rule called:

Grooming Is Better Than Gucci

Even if you have the wardrobe basics together, there is still a way to look a hot mess. If your grooming is sub-par, then you will just look like a well-dressed cave woman. Or to use a quote from the

Oscar-snubbed cinematic masterpiece Clueless, "You will look full on Monet." Meaning you'll look good from afar, but a mess up close.

As a realtor, you are up close and personal with clients and prospects, whether you are in a car driving a client/prospect to show a property, or in a walk-in closet showing them the recessed lighting. You need to look great both up close and at a distance.

The rule "grooming is better than Gucci" means that even if you are decked out in threads from a high-end designer, you will look a mess if you aren't properly maintaining yourself. It is a shame to be wearing $2,000 boots and still look like a 99¢ Store realtor. You can tell a lot about income brackets simply by looking at how well someone is maintained.

So here is the portion of the book where I tell you to only drink organically certified spring water, nibble on carrots all day, and find a way to fit two hours of exercise into each day. You'll have great skin and you'll be so thin that they will have to tie you down when the Santa Ana winds start to blow. Just kidding (now don't you feel bad for calling me a Bi*** after reading that paragraph).

All you need to know to have great style maintenance is to remember to be NEFT-Y.

N = Nails
E = Eyebrows
F = Facial hair
T = Teeth
Y = You know you need to do this, girl, so get off your duff and do it!

For each if the items, I will give you three different budget tiers and you can progress to a different budget level as you get closer and closer to Millionaire Real Estate Agent status. The first level when you are just starting out is called "Baller on a Budget." This is for when you know you have a ton of potential but your income has not yet matched your potential. There will be a lot of Do-It-Yourself items. Once you start making a little bit more money, you can progress to "Pampered Professional" and be able to splurge every now and then. "Maintained Millionaire" is for when money isn't an object and you can have standing appointments at the salon or any other beauty establishment.

N = Nails

If you are a girly-girl, then you want to keep your nails polished at all times. Now, depending on your preference and your budget, you can keep your nails short and do them yourself a home. Or you can go to a salon to get them done on a regular basis about every two weeks. Your nails should never be chipped and tacky and, of course, you want to have fresh polish for your most important events and meetings.

If you are not a girly-girl, you can forego the colored nail polish and just go with clear nail polish. It still looks stylish and professional.

Baller on a Budget: Do-it-Yourself. Get 2 to 3 different nail polish colors and plenty of nail polish remover. Make sure one of the colors you get is a red that compliments your skin tone. When you first try to paint your nails, they will look a mess. In fact with the red nail polish dripping down your hands, your coworkers may ask you if you won the bar fight last night. I promise you that practice makes perfect and the more you do it, the better you will get. People would have thought that I suffered from Parkinson's disease when I first started doing my own nails; now I could perfectly paint my nails while riding the newest roller coaster at Six Flags.

Pampered Professional: Not quite millionaire status, but on your way. Try to get your nails done for special occasions (manicures). If you have gel, acrylic, or anything else, you need to go every two weeks for touch-ups.

Maintained Millionaire: You can easily afford to get your nails done every two weeks and for special occasions. The nail salon is a great place to meet new clients and get referrals. As a regular, you'll have first dibs on clients.

E= Eyebrows

Oprah has been known to say that every time she gets her eyebrows arched, the press goes into a frenzy speculating that she got a face lift. Yes, sculpted eyebrows can make that big of an impact. Sculpted eyebrows help frame the face and can even help your face to look thinner and younger.

Eyebrows are very important. If professional make-up artists were asked which they would rather give up, their tweezers or their right arm, there would be many one armed makeup artists. As a wardrobe stylist, tweezers were always in the kit that I would take to the set, just in case.

There are many options for maintaining your eyebrows. You can wax, tweeze, or thread. Waxing, tweezing, and threading are all fairly inexpensive for eyebrows, unless you go to a high-end professional that specializes in eyebrows. Find a method that works best for you. The growth of your eyebrows will determine how often you need to go for touch-ups.

Baller on a budget: Pay to go to a professional to get your eyebrows done. Ask a ton of questions and then maintain your eyebrows yourself with a pair of tweezers. You just follow the shape that they originally created. If you have a low pain threshold, you may need to hold some ice on your brow before you tweeze. Or you can do like they did in the Wild West, get a bottle of whiskey and bite down on a stick while you tweeze. (That is not advisable if you still want to have eyebrows after your eyebrow grooming session.)

Pampered professional: You go on a regular basis to get your eyebrows touched up, and you know how to do a quick fix yourself if you are between appointments.

Maintained Millionaire: You have an eyebrow person. You had a consultation and the perfect eyebrow shape for you was determined. You eyebrows are always well-maintained.

A Note on YouTube

YouTube is a great resource for do-it-yourself grooming. Need to know how to achieve a perfect DIY manicure? Need to know how to arch your eyebrows? There is a YouTube video that will walk you through how to do it. It is a great grooming resource right at your fingertips. Technology is great... go nerds!!!

F = Facial Hair

It's elusive, but you've seen it. It's not quite as elusive as the Loch Ness monster, but we have probably all encountered the feminine mustache and found it so distracting that we couldn't even focus on the words that were coming out from below the mustache. Could you imagine having a property showing while wearing a mustache? You may be showing off the stainless steel appliances and the double oven, but your potential buyer is just thinking, "Mustache, mustache, mustache!!!"

You may have also seen the womanly beard, sideburns, or goatee. These are all extremely unattractive looks. The best way to deal with facial hair is waxing, as it will take longer for the hair to come in. Facial hair should be dealt with immediately!

Baller on a Budget: If you have to choose between getting your eyebrows waxed or your facial hair removed, choose facial hair. It can affect how your makeup behaves on your skin. You don't want people saying that your makeup looks fluffy.

Pampered Professional: Your facial hair is gardened on a regular basis. In fact you get your eyebrows and facial hair taken care of at the same time.

Maintained Millionaire: You may look into more permanent hair removal such as laser hair removal. Your face is free of facial hair and you look the essence of femininity.

T = Teeth

While I would never dare suggest that you go out and spend thousands of dollars on orthodontia, there are lower-cost options to improve your smile. Many people have said that your smile is your best accessory. If you are not completely happy with how straight your teeth are, you can at least have white slightly crooked teeth.

Consult with your dentist to determine which teeth-whitening option is best for you. Your dentist will also be able to tell you how often you can whiten your teeth without damaging them. Trust me, you will learn to love your smile even more with whiter teeth. Whiter teeth means more smiling, and happy people are attractive; your smile will be like a tractor beam pulling them in.

Baller on a Budget: There are many affordable over-the-counter options to whiten your teeth. You may even be able to find a coupon for it in your local newspaper or on sites such as Groupon.

Pampered Professional: You whiten your teeth annually, alternating between over-the-counter methods and your dentist.

Maintained Millionaire: You visit the dentist to regularly have your teeth whitened.

Y = You know you need to do this, girl, so get off your duff and do it!

This stuff is not fun, it is not sexy. In fact, this stuff can be down right painful. I am asking you to regularly get hair ripped from your body. You can ask any model and they will tell you that beauty is pain, but they are willing to endure the hair pulling, too tight shoes, and painful facials because they are getting paid to put up with it, so are you. You have to sell yourself in order to get the opportunity to work for your clients. You are your product just as much as the properties you list.

I know there will be days that you don't want to do this, and you may put it off. You may think there are better ways to spend your money, but this is an investment in you. If you want to be a millionaire real estate agent, you need to look like a million bucks!

Where Do I Find The Money For All Of This Style Maintenance?

It may seem like you need to have the income of a Hollywood actress in order to sustain all of this beauty work, but in actuality, this can be quite affordable.

Grooming Budget

The prices computed below are based on getting these services in San Diego, which can be a bit pricier than other parts of the country. These prices also include tips for the nail technician and esthetician, because you should be classy while you're getting beautiful.

Nails (maximum s2x per month)	$15.00
Eyebrows (1x per month)	$15.00
Facial hair waxing (1x per month)	$ 8.00
Teeth whitening (1x per year)	$ 2.92
Monthly total	$40.92 per month

So it is about $40 per month for style maintenance, and can be even cheaper if you do your nails yourself. While I know household budgets can be extremely tight, this isn't really a lot of money per month to make an investment in yourself and your career.

Could you sacrifice:

- ◊ 9 Big Mac's a month
- ◊ 10 Cafe Mocha's a month
- ◊ 25 songs on iTunes
- ◊ 5 ebooks on your Kindle
- ◊ Popcorn and a soda at the movies (ok, maybe not quite $40, but it seems like it)
- ◊ 4/50th of an iPhone
- ◊ 1/100th of a pair of Jimmy Choo shoes
- ◊ 6/100,000th of a 2013 Porsche Cayenne

See! You are not really sacrificing all that much. Think of it as an investment in you and your business.

What you'll need at home:

Equipment List

____ Nail Kit
____ Nail polish remover
____ 2-3 nail polish colors including a clear top coat
____ Cotton balls
____ Tweezers
____ Wax strips or hair remover (if applicable)
____ Teeth whitening kit (if applicable)

Nail Kit

You can get a nail kit from a pharmacy or discount super store such as Target or Wal-Mart. Or you can get a really pretty one if you go to cosmetic stores such as Ulta or Sephora. The nail kit will include items such as a nail file, cuticle pusher, nail clippers, etc. They often come in a very compact pouch or clutch. If you are searching for a nail kit online, you may also want to search for "Travel Nail Kit." Many nail kits also come with tweezers, so you will kill two birds with one stone.

If you decide to go with faux nails such as gel or acrylic then you do not need all of the nail equipment at home, but it is great to have in case you break a nail or get frustrated and decide to take your nails off (also known as PMS).

Beauty On The Go

There are few white collar professional positions that require being on the go like a real estate professional. You can often be found out of the office driving around town. Your car is very much your second office, so it is very important that you carry a travel beauty kit for your car for emergencies or when you are so busy that you are slacking on style maintenance. As you progress through the rest of the book, I'll give you other items you should include in your emergency beauty kit. For now, here are the items specifically related to this chapter:

- ◊ Travel nail kit - it will be extra small and perfect for travel
- ◊ Tweezers - of course
- ◊ A bottle of quick dry nail polish - great for quick nail touch ups, but also great for stopping runs in your pantyhose. (Many beauty supply retailers will have small sample bottles. These bottles are extra small and are perfect for travel.)

◊   Mints (although they can't instantly whiten your teeth, they are useful to help you feel confident in close corners with other people).

Professionals have kits too

The idea of having an emergency kit is not foreign to us in the beauty profession. As a wardrobe stylist, you have a kit and you have to bring it to the set or location. It contains everything you will need for emergencies, quick beauty fixes, and last minute wardrobe fixes. I have taken this great idea and adapted it for personal use, as I am often darting from one thing to the next and need to look great. If you think there is pressure to look good as a realtor, imagine what it is like to be known as a fashion expert (I sometimes wear a ball gown to take out my trash).

Emergency kit in the car or office?

Some of you may be thinking, why the car? Why not keep your beauty on-the-go kit in the office? Here's the rationale. If you are at the office, presumably your car is there also, therefore you have access to it. Not necessarily so, the other way around!

You can also have two kits—one at the office and in the car. If you are in a senior position at work, an extra office kit is a great toolbox for your other female colleagues. While not all items can be shared hygienically, they will appreciate the nail clippers, nail polish, and mints. Don't you want them also looking their best at all times?

As a wardrobe stylist, you have multiple kits. You have your big one that contains everything under the sun, and then you have another one slung around your shoulder or waist as a mini-purse or fanny pack. These are for when you need to be where the model is. When the model is on a small rock in the middle of an oceanic cove, you'd better have what you need when you need to make a wardrobe adjustment while having to wade through shallow ocean waters and climb barefoot onto a large rock. Having been through these types of experiences, I know what you need and where to put it to ensure you are covered for all emergencies.

If you are interested in learning more about style maintenance, then I'd like to recommend a great book, How to Look Expensive by Andrea Pomerantz. This is an excellent book to use to develop a beauty routine. She has great information on hair, skin, and cosmetics. There is a lot of information in the book. Don't get overwhelmed; just pick a few things to start doing and do them right away. Remember the "Y" of "NEFT-Y"—you know you need to do this, girl, so get off your duff and do it!

Above And Beyond

This chapter just covers the basic grooming, but if you were an A+ student and looking for ways to get extra credit, then you would love this section. There are several other areas of your appearance you may want to attend to in order to look like a million bucks. These areas are your hair, your make-up, and your skin. If you are not interested in going above and beyond, simply skip ahead to the end of the chapter for your end-of-chapter bonus.

Your Hair

Hair is often the toughest part for people. Women are notoriously particular about their hair, but remember hair grows back and color can be changed back fairly quickly. Now with the advances in extensions, you do not even have to wait for hair to grow back.

Did you know that you can have hair consultations? This is where you just meet with a hairdresser to discuss ideas about what you would like to do. Some hairdressers offer free consultations while others may charge you for it, but it's a great way to get some options and then take some time to think about what you would want to do.

Call your hairdresser and set up a consultation. A few days before your consultation, go online and find some hairstyles that you like and print them out. Also print out any hair colors that you like. Again, here it would be helpful to know your color seasons (see Chapter 4 for more information and color seasons) because you can look at celebrities that are in your season and see which hair colors look best on them. For example, if your season is winter, celebrities with your same color palette would be Salma Hayek, Anne Hathaway, Halle Berry, Penelope Cruz, and Catherine Zeta Jones.

During your hair consultation, your hairdresser should also discuss your face shape. Again, your hairstyle should create greater balance. If you have a round face, you do not want chin length hair, even if it is the hot style of the moment, because it is going to make your face look fuller than normal. You want something with some length to lengthen your face. Be sure to ask your hairdresser whether this or that style/length goes with your face shape.

If you don't have a hairdresser you really trust (and everyone should), talk to your friends, family, or colleagues whose hair you like and ask who their hairdresser is.

Before you take the plunge, you need to ask about maintenance. How often will you need to come to the salon for a cut and color? How long will it take you to do your hair in the morning? Also ask about what I call "unintended consequences."

I had a relative who dyed her hair jet-black. She should not have done this because she was more of an autumn and should have had some warmer brown tones in her hair. For the weekend she went with some friends to Six Flags Magic Mountain, an amusement park in the Los Angeles area of southern California. By the way, she did this in mid summer when the temperature was in the high 90's. While waiting in line for a roller coaster, she nearly fainted; she was not used to the darker color hair that attracts so much heat. She immediately wanted to change her hair color back, but black is one of the colors that can be hard to strip out. So she had to go around with this really dark hair that made her seem harsh and irritated, when she was actually one of the most bubbly and outgoing people I knew. The additional heat and inability to get rid of the black were unintended consequences, which leads me to another great question to ask your hairdresser: If you don't like this new style, what are your options afterward?

Are you bored with just wearing a ponytail? Get some other quick 10 minute or less style options. There are many websites out there with great hairstyles for every type of hair. From various websites, I have printed out 5 hairstyles and directions and put them in a file. I pull it out when I need something to do with my hair. I also have pictures on my computer, cell phone, and Pinterest. I refer to them often for hairstyle ideas.

A hairstyle that everyone needs to know how to do is called the "chignon." This is essentially a fancier bun. When models are going around to do castings, they are often told do this quick hairstyle. It instantly makes you look more pulled together. I also get the most compliments with this simple style. There are so many resources available online. This is my go-to hairstyle when I am fed up, and I get the most compliments when I wear my hair like this.

Makeup

I am someone who likes makeup a lot. The happiest place on earth to me is the MAC cosmetics counter, not Disneyland. Where makeup is concerned, everyone should use something (especially if you want to be a Millionaire Real Estate Agent). But you need to know what you like. It is important to consider whether you want to look extremely natural like you don't have on any makeup, or maybe you want to look like you are getting ready to step onto the main stage of the Golden Nugget. (I am toward the Golden Nugget end of the spectrum.)

I've worn makeup forever, but for the longest time I never had the look I wanted. Everyone always wanted to keep my makeup very natural. I had various "makeovers" by Avon, Mary Kay and other people...nothing against them personally, but it was never what I wanted. It never made me go "Wow, this is exactly what I wanted." Finally, I said I was just going to ask someone whose makeup I admired what she used and how she did her makeup. I asked one of my girlfriends whose makeup I had always admired. She said she used MAC, so I went to that store. I noticed all of the girls working in there had the makeup look I wanted. I had a makeover and I even took makeup classes from them. I became much happier with my makeup, and I can now achieve that look on my own.

The important thing is to find someone wearing the look you like and ask her how she achieved that look. Just because someone showed you how to do your eye makeup in 1985, does not mean that you have to stick with it if you do not like it. Do what I did, find someone wearing makeup that you like and ask her what she does. An important distinction is to note that you need to take into consideration your lifestyle. You need to know how much time you are willing to spend in the morning "putting on your face," and also whether you'll have time and are willing to do touch-ups throughout the day. There have been many innovations in cosmetics, such as primers you can apply under your makeup that make it stay perfect all day long.

If you are trying to be a Millionaire Real Estate Agent, I would say at the very minimum, you should have on mascara, blush, and tinted moisturizer to even out your skin tone. That is a perfectly chic makeup routine for the weekend.

Your Skin

If you are unhappy with your skin, help is available. Depending on the severity of your skin situation, you may want to consider consulting with a dermatologist to see what will work best with your skin type. Having great skin can save you a lot of time and money on cosmetics. There is less to cover up, and on the weekends you can still look great with nothing more than a tinted moisturizer.

If your skin is one of the things you are unhappy about, change it. There is no reason to continue to be unhappy with yourself when there are so many tools and resources available to help improve your situation. There are options available that are very soothing and even border on pampering. Learn to love your skin.

P.S. If you are concerned about skin discoloration, sun spots, or wrinkles, a consultation with a dermatologist may also be warranted. While they are not miracle workers, there are many safe, non-surgical options available. What can it hurt to have a consultation?

Energy

I know said that I was not going to speak to you about fitness and weight loss, and I will not. I know that in order for you to give up your peanut M&M's, I would have to pry them from your cold dead hands. However, I am going to talk to about your energy levels.

Growing a business/career to the million dollar level takes time and a significant amount of energy. I once had a mentor tell me that being an entrepreneur takes more energy than the average person uses. Being a kick-butt realtor is like being an entrepreneur—you are fully in charge of your own destiny. It is going to require a greater than average amount of energy, especially in the beginning. Implementing all of these changes to your appearance and sense of style can be a lot of work.

Exercise is a great way to increase and maintain your energy. These changes can also be accomplished with energy drinks, espresso, and only sleeping four hours a night. You can take any path that you like. And that completes my spiel on diet and exercise. Choose what works for you.

Even though I am a fashion expert and not a beauty expert, I have been fortunate enough to have spent time in front of the camera and behind the camera. In front of the camera, I know what kind of maintenance and grooming needs to be done to pull off a decent picture. But the real enlightenment has come from working behind the camera when working with inexperienced models or clueless clients. I know the basic things to discuss when booking models, to make sure they show up camera ready. I have had to have uncomfortable conversations with people explaining why some things may not be appropriate with the look we are going for. Everything from cheap hair extensions to unnatural looking colored contact lenses and various other things that make a model look more trashy than they were intending.

Those conversations are hard and I dread it every time I have to have one, but I always think, what would I want someone to do for me? I would want someone to tell me if there was a better way of doing things. While this chapter really touches on the very, very basic items, there are many things a maintained realtor could do to add a little extra polish to her image.

End-Of-Chapter Bonu$:

By now, you have probably realized that you need to have a beauty team to help you look millionaire marvelous. Your beauty team is a great source of clients and referrals, which is another great reason why you might want to splurge and go to a salon. The nicer the salon, the better the opportunities to network with people that can help you get to millionaire status.

Did you know you can put your beauty team to work for you just like your very own sales team? Here is how you can put them to work:

Make sure your hairdresser, nail tech, and esthetician know that you are a realtor and which geographic areas and types of realty you specialize in.

Give them some of your business cards—this process is much easier if you have really nice business cards that complement your style.

Be a good client and reciprocate—ask them for a stack of their business cards so you can help them with their business as well.

Be sure to ask on a regular basis, "Do you know anyone looking for a house?" or "Do you know anyone who is having trouble selling their house?" Sometimes you just need to jog people's memory and they are more than eager to help.

With those 4 steps, you have just built great referral sources that can send you people on a regular basis. Oh yeah—remember to tip well! Not only will it put you in their good graces, but it is also good karma for starting to allow the referrals to flow in.

CHAPTER 3

The Shapely Realtor

There is a very famous brand of jeans called "Rich & Skinny." If I could make an alternate title for this chapter, it would be called Rich and Skinny. This chapter is going to focus on how to make your clothes (and you) look more expensive. It is also going to help you look thinner—or at the very least more balanced and proportional, which will make you look thinner.

This chapter is all about fit and body shape. The thing that I love, love, love about well-made clothing is that it fits your body beautifully. You instantly look better. I remember that this lesson was really driven home during the fittings for my wedding dress. Everyone (salesgirls included) liked my dress when I first purchased it, but after it was fitted, everyone really loved it. After the fitting, my waist looked teeny tiny and everyone kept saying that I looked like a doll because the dress fit so perfectly and hugged all the right curves. The dress instantly looked a lot more expensive than it really was.

All of you married and divorced gals probably had similar experiences. You divorced gals may be trying to block out that painful memory, but remember the dress and let the memories of the ex-groom retreat to the nether regions of your mind that will only be retrievable via Ginkgo Biloba and excessive amounts of alcohol.

The 5 Basic Body Shapes

In chapter 4, we will discuss which season you are. From there, we will determine your color season, color palette, and your personal branding. In this chapter, we are going to determine your body shape. This will help you get to rich(er) and skinny(er). There are 5 basic body shapes. The way to determine your body shape is to look at the widest part of your body.

- You are an Apple if the widest part of your body is your mid section. You are probably most self conscious of your belly area.

- You are a Pear if the widest part of your body is your hips and/or thighs. Many women fit into this category. I personally want to start a support group for us. Beyonce is working over time to have us known as Bootylicious.

- You are an Upside Down Pear if the widest part of your body is your chest. Small breasted women hate when you walk into the room.

- You are a Ruler if there is no widest part of your body. You are pretty straight up and down with very few curves. Many times your shoulders may be the widest part on you. Many women envy you because of the way clothes fit on you.

- You are an Hourglass if the widest parts of your body are your chest and hips and/or thighs because they are the same width around. You have a very balanced body type. Many women also envy you because of the way clothes fit on you. I personally think you and rulers should be banished to the island of perfect bodies and stop making the rest of us feel bad (Rulers and Hourglasses, don't hold that against me—please continue to read the book!)

If you are still confused about which body type you are, then let's get ready to play the Celebrity Match Game, where you can see which group of celebrities your body type belongs to.

Apple body shapes
Melissa McCarthy
Amber Riley

Pear body shapes
Beyonce
Jennifer Lopez
Kristin Davis
Katie Holmes
Kim Kardashian

Upside down pear body shapes
Dolly Parton
Catherine Zeta-Jones

Ruler body shapes
Keira Knightly
Gwyneth Paltrow
Kate Bosworth
Kate Hudson

Hourglass
Jessica Simpson
Salma Hayek
Scarlett Johansson
America Ferrara

Now that you know w body shape you are, let's revisit the 12 Apostles of Style—this time with suggested tweaks based on your body type. I call this the 12 Apostles of Style Remix:

The 1st Apostle - The Ballet Flat

All body types can wear this style of shoes. However, if you have large calves, you want to be careful of wearing ballet flats with dresses and skirts. It can have the effect of making your legs look like tree trunks.

The 2nd Apostle - Men's White Shirt

Apple: Instead of a traditional button-up shirt, you may want to find one that has hook and eye closures all the way down instead of buttons. Make sure your shirt is always worn with the top few buttons/closures undone to create a nice v-neckline.

Upside Down Pear: You usually have trouble getting shirts to fit in the bust area. Get a shirt that fits in the bust area (meaning the buttons are not pulling). Then get the shirt taken in on the areas that do not fit, such as the shoulders or the waist. For most of us, clothes do not fit right off the rack; there is nothing wrong with having your clothes tailored to your body.

Ruler: Look for shirts that have pockets or paneling on the shirt.

Hourglass: You want to look for a shirt that is going to have a little stretch to it.

The 3rd Apostle - Cashmere Turtleneck or Sweater

Apple: Get a v-neck sweater instead of a turtleneck.

Ruler: Get a round-neck sweater as opposed to a turtleneck.

Hourglass: Get a v-neck sweater instead of a turtleneck.

The 4th Apostle - Trench Coat

Apple: If you are on the shorter side, the coat should end right above your knees.

Pear: To draw attention away from your butt, hip, and thighs, you want to wear the coat one of two possible ways. The first is to wear it open—it will actually make a vertical line down your thigh, making it appear thinner. The second way is to wear it closed and belted so the focus is on your waist. Make sure to get a trench coat with a great belt.

Ruler: A 3/4 length coat is a great option for you...it shows just enough leg.

The 5th Apostle - The Little Black Dress

Apple: Look for a dress with an empire waist to disguise your belly. You can ask the sales person at the store or search for that term when shopping online.

Pear: Look for an A-line dress that will skim over any real (or imaginary) saddlebags.

Upside Down Pear: Look for a shallow V neckline.

Ruler: A bias cut dress will help you create curves - just asks the sales person at the store or search for that term online to find the perfect LBD for you.

Hourglass: Look for a dress that will help elongate your short waist.

The 6th Apostle - Classic Black High Heels

This works for all body types.

The 7th Apostle - Diamond Earrings

This works for all body types—bling bling, ladies!

The 8th Apostle - Suit

Apple: Choose a jacket with heavy tailoring to help create a waist for you.

Upside Down Pear: Avoid double-breasted jackets.

Hourglass: A two-button jacket is a great option for you.

The 9th Apostle - Jeans

Apple: You might want to get jeans with flaps on the back pockets to create the illusion of a plumper booty.

Pear: Straight-leg or boot cut are going to be great options for you.

Upside Down Pear: You might want to get jeans with flaps on the back pockets to create the illusion of plumper booty.

Hourglass: You might need to fit your hips and then have the waistline taken in.

The 10th Apostle - Pearl Necklace

This works for all body types.

The 11th Apostle - Pencil Skirt

Apple: Look for side-fastening and a flat front. You do not want to create any extra bulk around your midsection.

Pear: You can also get an A-Line skirt if you are self-conscious in a pencil skirt.

Hourglass: This skirt is perfect for your body type.

The 12th Apostle - Cardigan

Apple: Look for a shallow v neckline

Upside down pear: Look for a shallow v neckline

Ruler: Look for a cardigan with a rounded neckline

Hourglass: Look for a neckline with v neckline

You Don't Need To Break The Bank

There is an old joke that asks the question, "How do you get to Carnegie Hall?" The answer is "practice, practice, practice."

In real estate we might ask the question, "What is the key to success?" The answer is "location, location, location".

With style, the key to your success is "fit, fit, fit!!!"

Maybe you don't have the budget for a designer suit. Even if you don't have the finances for a top-of-the-line suit, you have $20 to $40 to get your suits altered, and that will make you look like a million bucks!

A common mistake I see women make is that when they start making a little bit of money, they go out and buy a designer suit. All designers are not created equal. Just because something has a designer label, it is not necessarily stylish. You can't buy taste. It makes me so frustrated that sometimes I just want to scream!

A lot of times, you can go out and buy a cheaper, more stylish suit and have it tailored, and you will wear it better than the woman who spent $2,000 on a suit just because of the designer label even though it doesn't flatter her at all.

Sometimes you have to "do what you can with what you got." We all have $20 to $40 to get items fitted. Use what you got!

Here is another little secret I will let out of the bag:

The reasons that model looks so good in photo shoots is that we alter her clothes all the time using whatever we have on set. If you were to turn a model around on set, you would see safety pins and binder clips "altering" the garment so that it clings to her body in all the right places!

I often thought of taking the photos in my portfolio and writing notes so clients can see what was going on behind the scenes in photo shoots. We understand that a well-fitted garment makes the look. In almost every photo, I have altered the garment in some way that is not visible because of the camera angle.

People's careers may be on the line in the effort to get a great shot. Your career is on the line every time you step out the door in a less than fabulous ensemble. Let's improve the odds of you stepping into opportunity. Remember fit, fit, fit!

A Cheat Sheet On Looking Slimmer

Get a new bra. We hear this all the time, but never do anything about it. Go to a boutique lingerie shop or high-end department store to get measured for a bra. You want to go somewhere that the sales people have a lot of training in measuring bra sizes. Lingerie shops that can be found in every mall in America do not necessarily have the same training. A correct fitting bra will hold your breasts up in their right place giving you a waist and, according to a recent study, can help you look 10 pounds slimmer!

Get a body shaper. The most popular brand on the market is Spanx, but a body shaper can now be found in almost any store and under many fashion brands. There are now body shapers that can go from your tummy all the way down to your ankles. The good news is that this body shaper technology has now made its way into underwear. Body shapers can now become a staple of your wardrobe and not just for special occasions. The various makers of body shapers attest to the fact that they can make you look 10 - 15 pounds slimmer.

Get a new hairstyle. Even your hairstyle may be against you. You may need to get your hairstyle updated, especially if you have gained weight recently. That hairstyle might have been fine 20 pounds ago, but now it is making you look puffier than you are. A slimming hairstyle can shave another few pounds off of your appearance.

Buy dark colored clothes. Disguises are not only for secret agents. You can also disguise your problem areas by dressing them in dark colors. If you are bigger on the bottom, you want to have dark-colored clothing on the bottom. If you are top-heavy, you want to have darker clothing on the top. To make this work, you also need lighter-colored clothes for the areas you are not trying to minimize.

Buy "wow" jewelry. Take a cue from master magicians and become versatile in the art of misdirection. A well-placed necklace can bring the eye upward. It also says, "Don't look at the jiggle... quick, look over here... something shiny."

Buy a pair of high heels. Liposuction in the form of a stiletto. High heels help you look taller and thinner, always. However, if you have thick calves or "cankles" avoid ankle straps, it draws attention to the thickness happening around your feet.

Book Recommendations

If you want to learn even more about how to dress slimmer, there are several books that I would recommend.

How to Never Look Fat Again by Charla Krupp is one of the best books on the subject because she breaks it down by body feature. For example, what not to do if you have big calves, or broad shoulders, or a muffin top. You get to know just a few of these rules and it will transform the way you look in your clothes. I don't expect you to dissect and memorize everything in the book like a professional has to, but just a handful of the tips well-implemented will put you on your way to Rich and Skinny.

The Wow Factor: Insider Style Secrets for Every Body and Every Budget by Jacqui Stafford is another great book. The different body types she has in the book are a slight variation from the ones I have in this book. However, there are some great tips for specific items of clothes. For example, she gives specific tips by body type for a bathing suit.

Your New BFF... Body Shapers

You may know them as girdles or corsets. You may even know them as a specific brand name such as Spanx. Regardless, body shapers are your friends. If you do not own one, I would suggest that you at least go try one on. You will see what a difference they make and become enticed by them. Some of you will be turned off by them, because you will say that they are uncomfortable. If they are truly uncomfortable, then maybe try a size up. However, I'm not going to lie to you. A pair of Spanx is not going to feel like your favorite pair of sweat pants at home. However, they can make you feel more comfortable in your skin and thus make you more confident.

If, when you are dressed up, you feel a little self-conscious and are constantly pulling and tugging on your clothes, a body shaper can be a great way to allay your fears that something is exposed or jiggling too much. For this reason alone, you may want to wear one. I have had clients who are in great shape and don't really need a body shaper, but I noticed they are more relaxed and themselves when they have one on.

I personally like body shapers for a lot of dress-up events because they make your clothes lie much nicer on you; they're not necessarily just to hold in fat. You don't have to have one, but I would say give it a try before you decide. You may even become obsessed with them, like a relative of mine who wore two pairs of Spanx so that she would look nice in her dress. We almost had to cut her out of them (If you are reading this, you know who you are, and yes—I am talking about you!)

Let Me Introduce You To Your Worst Nightmare

Most of us are not extremely happy when there is a work event we must attend. You have to dress up and be around people that you may or may not like. Let's be realistic, how many of your work colleagues would you be hanging out with if you had not met them through work? You have more important things you could be doing, like watching a marathon of Breaking Bad on Netflix. So step 1 to making this your nightmare is that it is an office party or some other similar function.

Now imagine that the work party was a pool party. We are just imagining—no need to start writing your suicide note. What advice does a style guru have for navigating a professional pool party?

Hire a body double

Fake skiing accident from the prior weekend and show up in regular clothes and a fake cast

Convert to Islam and wear a burka

Just find a great cover-up to wear and be so interesting, funny, and fabulous that no one notices that they haven't seen you dive into the pool in a bathing suit

Body Shape Q & A

Q: I'm an Apple shape; what is the number one thing I could do to appear slimmer?

A: The number one thing you could do is get fitted for a bra and get a bra that really fits; it is going to help you look like you have a longer torso and a waist. This is the first thing I would do if I were an apple body shape.

Q: Other body shapes seem to have some advantages. I'm a pear shape; what is great about being a pear shape?

A: You get to wear strapped and strapless dresses and tops. Of course, this is especially true if you have nice toned arms.

Q: I am petite. Is there a trick for making me look taller?

A: Monochromatic dressing will help you look taller. This means dressing in one color or tone from head-to-toe. It creates one long line and will make you seem taller.

Q: Any other tricks for looking taller and slimmer?

A: Yes posture. Standing up straight helps you look taller and slimmer, and helps you look more confident. Image consultants are trained to teach you correct posture because it is important in how you carry yourself. There are also exercises that help you to have better posture. Additionally, Pilates and yoga are known for helping to improve posture.

Q: If there was one rule you or tip you could have everyone memorize, what would it be?

A: It would be, "Use dark colors to hide, and bright colors to emphasize." For example, if I am self-conscious about my thighs, I should wear black jeans and a white t-shirt. I wear the dark colors on the body areas I want to hide, and draw focus to where I want it by using brighter colors (the white t-shirt).

A Client's Story

I was working with a new photographer on a photo shoot. He had this great concept of a model standing on a rocky beach wearing dresses that kind of blow in the wind. It was a very dark and beautiful concept because the beach and sky were going to be dark and gloomy (with some creative photoshopping) and it was going to be juxtaposed with these exquisitely beautiful dresses.

We had been hunting for a great model for this shoot and found the perfect one—she had a great portfolio. We had never seen her in person, we had only communicated via email and phone. However, when we started communicating about the particulars of the photo shoot and I asked her for her size and shoe size she was a size 9. While a size 9 is perfectly fine in the real world, in the modeling world a size 9 is almost moving into plus size model territory. (I must insert here that a size 9 is not big. I have worked with real people who are a size 24 with great results). We were a little concerned because in her portfolio photos she did not look like a size 9.

She explained to us that she'd had a baby 4 months prior. I said I could work with a size 9. The girl is gorgeous. She is a new mom; let's do this. While shopping, I made sure to shop for items that would help to slim her and make sure that if she still had a little bit of a belly it wouldn't be a problem. We had several looks planned, and one dress arrived with only seconds to spare (I'm sure Fedex was tired of me calling and asking about this package).

The day of the photo shoot, we put the dresses on her, I pinned them in the all the right places, and she looked fantastic. We were even making jokes about how every woman is going to hate her if they see these photos and find out that she had a baby 4 months before. She looked great in all of her dresses and she was very happy with the outfits. She was so happy with her looks that she even posted a testimonial on my website, StyleRecipeCards.com

This photo shoot ended in success because I knew how to dress her body type. I knew what her perceived problem areas were and how to disguise them. I also did some really unique things with accessories to draw focus to other places. The problem that I see is that people unintentionally draw attention to the wrong places. So when someone brags about how much they spent on a dress or a top, I'm thinking, "Just because it is designer or expensive does not mean it is a good choice for you, and you look 15 pounds heavier than you really are." The reason that they have poor body image is because of their clothes. If they could see their real body they would have a lot more confidence.

End-Of-Chapter Bonu$:

This chapter is all about fit, so for this End of Chapter Bonus, we are going to translate the idea of fit over to your clients. Now that your clothes are fitting perfectly and you look like a million bucks, we need to find clients that fit and are worthy of you.

I want you to think of the best client you have had so far. You can use your own judgment to decide what you consider to be your "best" client. The best client can be the client with the largest transaction, the quickest close, the client that gave you the most referrals, or the client that was the easiest to work with. Your goal is to find more of these clients that are a good fit for you.

List the characteristics of your best client. What were the vital statistics—age, sex, marital status, where they lived, occupation, size of household, etc... Use the space below to list these characteristics:

The characteristics that you listed above are what you need to look for in new clients. Did your best client live in a certain suburb? If so, how can you reach more clients in that suburb? Was your best client a CPA? If so, how can you reach more CPA's in your territory?

Use the space below to brainstorm ideas on how you can target clients that meet the various characteristics:

Now you can use your new image and color-coordinated marketing materials (discussed in Chapter 4) to actively market to these people that are a perfect fit for you and your business.

CHAPTER 4

The Vibrant Realtor

Imagine being on stage in an auditorium filled with thousands of people and a spotlight's shining brightly in your face. Suddenly a microphone is thrust in your face and you are asked to answer the question, "When was the last time you failed and how did you handle it?"

Most of us would be tempted to answer that question with the response, "Now, and I am going to handle it by running off the stage and jumping through the nearest window, Cowardly Lion Style."

This is the exact scenario that pageant contestants have to deal with while wearing a wide smile on their faces. Many people don't know that the pageant actually begins long before the actual show. The girls have to make appearances and set themselves apart.

So of course, here I come to help a contestant in the Miss California pageant. There was a press event and she needed a great outfit. I did what I did best—I went shopping. I hit up some boutiques in downtown San Diego, put together some outfit boards, and sent them over for her for approval.

This was easier said then done. She looked at the first choice and said, "This outfit is black and white and one of the girls has already chosen this color palette." She looked at the next photo and said,

"Another girl is doing red—I can't do red." This went on for several outfits. I thought I was going to have to hit the pavement again in search of color that no one had ever seen before. I was about to hop on the phone with the Crayola Research and Development department when she finally found one that might work. It was a unique color combination of coral and turquoise. Hallelujah!

The weekend of her event, I picked up the outfit, prepped it, and had several accessory options ready. When the pictures of the event came back, they looked great. In every photo it was like "Pop! Here I am!" She looked great and stood out in a sea of girls. Mission Accomplished! She was able to differentiate herself.

That exact color palette and a similar outfit graced the cover of People Style Watch the next month. I sent her a copy of the cover with the note "See, we were ahead of the trend!"

I wanted to start this chapter with this story because it illustrates the importance of color. You may not be a pageant contestant (thank God—can you imagine having to wear a bathing suit on stage while people judge you? I think I had that nightmare once...), but you are competing all the time. You need to learn how to stand out from a sea of other realtors. If you've been out in the field long enough, you know it is tough. You don't have to worry about someone putting itching powder in your bikini bottom, but you do have to worry about someone else getting the listing, or someone else getting the referral or recruiting the best realtors.

Do You Know What Colors Look Good On You?

Sauerkraut, the Berlin Wall, and the Third Reich. Okay, so maybe everything from Germany has not been great, but Johannes Itten, the German colorist, did bring something great into the world. He popularized the practice of seasonal colors.

You have probably heard someone say, "I'm a winter" or "I'm a summer." If you have heard those phrases, the person is referencing

The German. He determined that everyone falls into 4 categories—Winter, Autumn, Spring, and Summer. Your season will help determine what colors best compliment you.

There is a full process you can go through called a color analysis to determine your best colors. This is usually done with a professional and you get very detailed information on the best colors for you. It is something to consider doing down the road.

However, this is a book, so we are going to cheat a little. We are going to do it the cheap and dirty way so that you can get some quick answers. In order to do that, we are going to play the Celebrity Match Game (envision a cheesy theme song every time you read the words Celebrity Match Game).

So reader, step right up and let me tell you the rules of the game. With this game, you are going to try to match yourself to the group of celebrities that have similar coloring to you. That means the celebrities that have similar eye color, hair color, and skin color. You will probably not find a perfect match, but you want to find the group that is closest to you.

GROUP A
Lindsay Lohan
Nicole Kidman
Blake Lively
Jennifer Aniston
Gisele Bundchen

GROUP B
Gwyneth Paltrow
Reese Witherspoon
Scarlett Johansson
Taylor Swift
Amanda Seyfried
Amy Adams
Reba McEntire

GROUP C
Jennifer Lopez
Cindy Crawford
Jennifer Love Hewitt
Lana Del Rey
Jessica Alba
Beyonce

GROUP D
Halle Berry
Naomi Campbell
Catherine Zeta-Jones
Mila Kunis
Anne Hathaway
Katy Perry
Lucy Liu

Have you chosen which you best fit into? Are you an A, B, C, or D? Go to the end of the book and turn to Appendix D to find out if you are Winter, Autumn, Spring, or Summer. Then turn back to this page and read about your season.

So You're a Winter

There is nothing cold and frigid about you. Winter has the boldest palette of colors to choose from. Oh, how I wish I was a winter! You have a great assortment of colors that look great on you.

FAB COLORS FOR YOU:
Stark White
Hot Pink
Red
Hunter Green
Navy

Grey
Black

DRAB COLORS FOR YOU:
Beige
Camel

SAMPLE POWER OUTFIT:
A great power outfit for a Winter would be an extremely tailored red pants suit with a black satin blouse and a pair of black high heels. Don't forget the black jeweled brooch.

SAMPLE WORK CASUAL OUTFIT:
Wear your red suit pants with your white men's button down shirt (#1 Apostle of Style). Accessorize with a thin navy belt and navy high heels.

So You're an Autumn

Dying vegetation is not what this color palette is about. If you have ever happened upon a cluster of trees in the middle of its autumnal transformation, you know that it is breathtaking. You will be just as breathtaking when you display your colors.

FAB COLORS FOR YOU:
Burgundy
Orange
Moss Green
Beige
Camel
Gold
Dark Brown

DRAB COLORS FOR YOU:
Most pastels

SAMPLE POWER OUTFIT:

A great power outfit would be a burgundy long-sleeved sheath dress, with brown high heels and a chunky gold necklace. Take the outfit over the top by accessorizing with a gold cuff bracelet or gold and burgundy earrings.

SAMPLE WORK CASUAL OUTFIT:
Be workplace chic in a camel colored calf-length pencil skirt, a white tank top with an emerald green cardigan (#12 Apostle of Style) over it. Complete the look with your small diamond (or faux diamond) earrings.

So You're a Spring

Put a spring in your step if you are a Spring. You color palette is light and fresh with a dusting of happiness. So hop, dive, and spring into your new color palette.

FAB COLORS FOR YOU
Peach
Golden Yellow
Camel
Golden Brown
Bright Blues

DRAB COLORS FOR YOU
Reds with blue undertones

SAMPLE POWER OUTFIT

A fierce golden brown skirt suit with a bright blue top. Accessorize with a long gold pendant necklace and matching golden brown high heels. Elevate the style even more with gold earrings.

SAMPLE WORK CASUAL OUTFIT:
A golden yellow summer dress with your golden brown suit jacket over it and matching brown heels. Complete the outfit with a cream/off white handbag.

So You're a Summer

Muy caliente! The summer color palette is not so much spicy as it is filled with very feminine pastels that calm and soothe. But be warned, this is the most delicate palette and requires more attention.

Fab Colors For You
Rose Pink
Soft Blues
Navy
Lavender
Plum
Rose-Brown

Drab Colors For You
Orange

Sample Power Outfit

A soft and simple power outfit would be a light grey tailored pant suit with a pastel pink bow tie blouse (a bow tie blouse is one where you can tie a small bow tie at the neckline). You can complete it with matching gray heels and gray pearl earrings.

Sample Work Casual Outfit

A sky blue and white print skirt, white top, and your light gray suit jacket. Wear with your pearl necklace (#10 Apostle of Style). Complete with a matching gray leather envelope clutch purse.

Create Easy Outfits

As you get more successful, you will be busier and will need to find ways to save time. A huge time saver is simply organizing your closets and drawers for easy mix-and-match to put together stylish outfits. This is even more important if you have not yet reached the millionaire real estate agent status and have a limited wardrobe. Your ability to mix and match is going to save you and your bank account in the beginning.

One way to accomplish this is by organizing your closet and drawers by color. Unless you are one of the rare people who enjoy living in chaos, your closet has some structure to it. At the very least, most people group like items together. Your coats are in one place and your jeans are in another. Now, most of our closets do not look like they could be in the Container Store catalog. I'm not saying that your closet should look like it could be on the cover of OCD Weekly, but let's add one more element of organization to your closet...color.

If possible, group your clothes together by color, meaning put all your red tops together and all your black pants together. Just by grouping by color, you will be able to put together great outfits.

Unless you are a true fashionista, you don't spend all day thinking about your clothes and how to mix and match them—unlike me. I do devote a significant about of time to clothes. Whenever someone invites me out, my first thought is, "What I am going to wear?" This thought happens before it occurs to me to ask for the date, time, and location of the event.

I hear that someone announces they are getting married, and I immediately think, "What am I going to wear?"

I hear the newscaster announce that the zombie apocalypse has occurred and I think, "As a zombie, will I have to wear tattered clothing? That is so been there, done that."

I totally get it. I am at the extreme end of the spectrum. Given that, I am going to give you an easy tip to mix and match outfits together so that you are not preoccupied with making outfits. I mean, someone needs to define the new zombie-chic look, everyone else will be too busy trying to find brains to eat.

Here's the tip:

Think of the last time that you got complimented on your outfit or item of clothing. Can you remember what you were wearing? Most likely you got the compliment because the color you were wearing was extremely flattering on you.

Now go to your closet and see what other outfits you can put together that include those colors. This process should be easy to do, if you have grouped together your clothing by color.

Here's how the thought process should go:

◊ "The last time I received a compliment, I was wearing olive green and gray."

◊ "Those must be great colors on me and/or a great color combination together."

◊ "What other outfits can I put together using olive green and gray?"

◊ This line of questioning leads perfectly into the next item of discussion…

Your Color Story

Let's talk marketing, and in particular, let's talk about marketing you and your business with color. Even though this book is about fashion and girly things, the end goal is to boost your income. In order to do that, you need to do some great marketing, and color can help.

Most realtors will fall into two groups: you either work for a company, or you are independent. If you are independent, you could be working for your own company and have people working under you, but since you do not have a boss (with the exception of extremely bossy clients), we will consider you independent.

If you work for a real estate firm

If you work for a real estate firm, then you probably already have company colors. Your company already has a brand. Your part of your color story has already been created. You have always been conscious that you were going to be surrounded by these company colors.

In research for this book and from client consultation, the thing that I commonly see is that women are unaware that their photo is going to be surrounded by certain colors. Meaning, they wear a bright green for their professional headshot not realizing that their company colors are red and black, so they end up looking like a Christmas tree on their company's website and on their business cards. That is the worst.

So if you work for a firm, when you are making decisions about your color palette, you want to always look great when you are surrounded by your company's marketing materials. I mean, are you really going to march into your boss's office and say, "I'm a summer. The company colors clash with my complexion, so I would like to put in a request to have our colors changed to pale yellow."

Once your boss finishes laughing, you may be pointed to the door. Here's a better strategy:

◊ Look at which colors are listed as fab colors for you.
◊ Pair each one with your company's colors and see which one compliments it the best.
◊ Pow! You've just created your color palette.

For example, say you are a Spring and your company colors are navy and white. You may think that you would then go with the bright blues, not necessarily. The golden yellow would make a beautiful addition to the company color palette.

So if I were creating your custom color palette, it would be white/cream, navy/aqua, golden yellow, and camel.

Why white/cream?

The company color is white. Cream is a much better color for a Spring, so one of the colors in your color palette would be cream, a slightly softer and warmer white.

Why navy/aqua?

The company color is navy, which is too harsh for a Spring, but an aqua color is perfect for a spring. Aqua is still in the blue family, so it makes the cut.

Why golden yellow?

Golden is one of the fab colors on a woman who is a Spring. It also makes a great accent to the navy and white. Can you picture the business card? A navy and white with a gorgeous picture of a woman dressed in yellow on it. It makes a striking impression.

Why camel?

I usually like to have at least 4 colors when creating a palette for someone so they have even more mix and match options. Camel was chosen because it is a color close to the golden yellow and it was also in the list of fab colors.

Now, do all of these colors go together? Of course they do; check this out. Use the chart below to mix and match outfits. Does a cream top go with an aqua skirt? Of course it does, it's modern. Choose a color for your top and choose a color for the bottoms. Trace your finger along the quadrants to see how to put an outfit together.

	Cream Top	Aqua Top	Golden Yellow	Camel Top
Cream Skirt	Gorgeous! A monochromatic look. Break it up with a navy or camel colored belt and matching shoes.	Stunning!	Cheery & Chic!	Stylish!
Aqua Skirt	Modern!	Fabulous! Break up the single color by having the top in an aqua and white print.	Color blocking! It's tricky to pull this one off.	Cultured!
Golden Yellow Skirt	Refreshing!	Killer Color Combo!	Sunny with a side of style. Add a tan braided belt and tan wedges.	Elegant!
Camel Skirt	Polished!	Sleek!	Classic!	Mono-chromatic chic! Accessorize well to pull of this ultra-sophisticated look.

Your custom color palette will help set you apart and will help establish your signature look. It will help you when you are shopping, because you can just go browse the sections that contain your color palette. It allows you to ignore a large portion of the store.

It will also help you save money. You won't buy clothes that don't go with anything in your wardrobe. It will also prevent you from buying things that are not the most flattering for you. The sad truth is that we waste a significant amount of money clothes because we buy things that don't work for us. We might as well go into the nearest casino and place a pile of money on black and hope we will come out a winner. If you could just take those wasted dollars and invest it in clothing that works for you, you could be light years ahead in your confidence and career.

No more gambling at the mall! Determine your color palette and invest wisely.

If you are independent or you own your own real estate company

If you are independent, congratulations! It takes a lot of hard work and courage to strike out on your own. In creating your own color palette, you have a lot more freedom. If you own your own company, then you have already determined your company colors and if you are not looking to change those, then just refer to the section, "If you work for a real estate firm." However, if you are looking to revamp everything, then we are starting from scratch and there are no other colors that you have to use as a jumping off point for your personal color palette.

If you are creating the color palette for your company, more than likely you are the star of the company or you are the face of the company even if there are several realtors working under you. Therefore, there are two questions I would ask first:

◊ What are my favorite colors?

◊ What colors look best on me?

The first question, what are your favorite colors, is fairly obvious. It is your company and you can do what you want. The second question, what colors look best on me, can be answered by using the materials in this book to determine what season you are. Then you can look at the list of fab colors provided for your season and choose colors. You can also get a more in-depth and comprehensive color analysis; be a professional. Since this involves marketing and branding your company, it may be a worthwhile investment to invest in a professional color analysis.

From answering the questions above, you should have narrowed down your list of colors to about 3 to 5 colors.

There are also a second set of questions I would ask to determine my personal/company color palette. Here are the two additional questions I would ask:

- ◊ What do these colors mean?
- ◊ What are the colors of my closest competitors?
- ◊ What do these colors mean?

Colors have meaning. Color can change people's moods. It can make them hungrier, thirstier, and it can elicit a variety of different emotions. Therefore, it is worth your time to see which emotions are tied to the colors you selected.

- ◊ Black: sophistication, mystery, and death
- ◊ Grey: stability, authority, and maturity
- ◊ Yellow: joy, energy, and caution
- ◊ White: freshness, hope, and coolness
- ◊ Red: excitement, passion, and danger
- ◊ Blue: peace, calmness, and affection
- ◊ Purple: royalty, dignity, and magic
- ◊ Pink: romance, faithfulness, and sensitivity
- ◊ Green: life, healing, and safety
- ◊ Orange: cheerful, sociable, and self-indulgent
- ◊ Brown: wholesome, practical, dull

There is further research that can be found by spending a romantic evening between you and Google. Light some candles, pour a glass of wine, and dive into color psychology using a search engine for research. This process will help you eliminate some of the 3 to 5 colors you have chosen.

What are the colors of my closest competitors?

This question is super-important because this is how you can stand out in the super-crowded real estate marketplace. Your closest competitors are the ones that look the most similar to you—meaning every real estate firm in your area is technically your competitor, but not your closest competitor. For example, if your firm specializes in the luxury home market, then your closest competitors are the firms that also specialize in the luxury home market in your area.

Generally, realtors stake claim to a certain area so that they can know it inside and out. Your competitor is the person that also has houses listed on the same block as you. Many of you know who your closest competitors are. If you don't, find out fast and establish a way that you are different (that really is a whole other marketing discussion in and of itself).

Through this process, you should have determined your company colors. Now, you need to determine your personal color palette; you usually want your color palette to include 4 to 6 colors.

To determine your personal color palette, go through the process outlined in the section, "If you work for a real estate firm." For the company colors, you are going to use the company colors you just created.

The great part of working for yourself is that you are not subject to the taste of someone else; however, it is more work, as you have probably figured out from reading the section above.

Actresses Do This Too

The idea of creating color palettes is used often in the entertainment field, particularly in movies and TV shows. The wardrobe and color palette are determined for a character, and a talented wardrobe artist changes the color palette as the character is involved in the script. A wardrobe artist helps create the character and story arch.

For example, in romantic comedies or chic flix, you'll notice that the color palette usually lightens over the course of the film. As the character falls in love, the colors get lighter and more feminine, as does the wardrobe. They will usually mix in more dresses, skirts, and other girly elements like lace, ruffles, satin, or sheer materials.

The actresses' color palette is changed over the course of the film because it is subliminally communicating to the audience, just like a great musical score can. These tricks should not just be limited to the elite in Hollywood. Everyday people and everyday realtors should be able to subliminally use colors to communicate to the marketplace.

Hopefully after nearing the end of this chapter, you realize why color is so important and you are excited to create your custom color palette. You can also see how a little effort put up front can save you a lot of time in your daily life. It will make it easier to go shopping and easier to mix and match outfits every day. You may still find it overwhelming to create a color palette and plan out a wardrobe. There are professionals you can reach out to that can affordably help you with that. After reading this chapter, you will be more skilled when dealing with professionals...you will not give up all your power over to them, and you can work together to co-create looks for becoming a Millionaire Real Estate Agent.

This chapter is great for providing a foundation to creating a color palette and getting pieces to help you mix n' match; however, to really achieve the look you are going for you will need to create many, many looks. This can be accomplished with just a few pieces. Trust me, I have had to work on projects with teeny, tiny budgets and had to make magic happen. What I typically see clients still do is get the few wardrobe pieces but know only a few ways of putting them together. The best feeling is when I show clients 5, 10, 15, or even 20 different ways to wear something (sometimes I like to challenge myself and see how many I can really make). When I first got into styling, a mentor told me the best thing to do is just keep practicing. All that practice has made me able to enjoy seeing how far a client's wardrobe can stretch.

End-Of-Chapter Bonu$:

Now that you have figured out your color palette, we need to address your marketing—or more specifically, your marketing materials. You've spent a lot of time determining which colors are the most flattering for you and your business. Even so, you are not a beauty pageant contestant. You need to stake your claim on your color palette, so let's get started.

Here is your marketing checklist:

___ Business Cards

___ Postcards

___ Website

___ Social Media profiles

___ Professional photo

___ Pens

___ Stationary

___ Email signature

___ Blog

___ Resume

___ Logo

___ Phone

Business Cards

Of course, your business cards should be in your color palette. If you work for a real estate firm, then you have to use their company cards with their company colors. However, your photo on the card should be in your personal color palette. If you followed the steps outlined in chapter 3, then your personal color palette should blend with your company colors perfectly.

Postcards

Postcards are an important marketing tool for Realtors. Make sure the postcards you send out are branded with your colors as well.

Website

This is a biggy. According to studies conducted by the National Association of Realtors, 82% of all home buyers begin their search online. You want your website to be branded to match all your other marketing materials. This helps people to see you as dependable with exceptional attention to detail.

Social Media Profile

"Look me up on Facebook." We have all heard that phrase before. Often times, people may be reluctant to exchange phone numbers or email, but will be perfectly happy to connect via various social media channels.

Make sure your cover photos are branded with your colors, and that your profile picture is one of you looking great in your personal color palette. For your personal social media accounts, you may not need to have the brand. For your company, however, for sure you want them branded.

Also, as a Realtor there is little distinction between your personal and professional life. The people that are in the various circles of your personal life are also your clients and referral sources. So at the very least, on your personal social media accounts I would have your professional headshot as your profile picture. This brands your profile picture with your personal color palette.

An additional caveat: be careful of the photos and information you share on these accounts. You would hate for a client to come across a photo of you dancing on top of a table with a lampshade on your head.

Professional Photos

You should know that your professional headshot should include you in your personal color palette. I know that I have said this several times before in this chapter, but I thought I should say it again, just in case you skipped ahead to the end of the chapter.

Pens

Often, real estate firms will have their own pens. These pens have the company name/realtor name and phone number on them. These pens are often brought out at events and open houses when potential buyers need to fill out the information. The hope is that these potential buyers will take the pen home and remember you or your company when they are in the market for a realtor.

These pens should not only have your name on them, but they should also be branded in your colors.

Stationery

I hope to God you have your own stationery. At the very least, you should have thank you cards. Fashion expert and author Nina Garcia agrees. In her book, The One Hundred: A Guide to the Pieces Every Stylish Woman Must Own, item number 57 on the list is monogrammed stationary.

Budget Friendly option - buy cards at Target or a similar store, but try to get them in your color palette

Mid-Range options - go online and find cards that exactly match your color palette

Millionaire options - go online and order your own personal cards with your name on them and in your own custom color palette. Nothing screams class and elegance as custom thank you cards. Actually, class and elegance don't scream, they whisper delicately and command everyone's attention.

Email Signature

I once sold a property in another state all through email and phone conversations, so I know that email is an essential tool for a realtor. Use your email signature to also help market yourself. Make sure your email signature includes your name, company, phone number. I also put social media links in my email signature, but that may not be for everybody.

Make sure your email signature is branded with your company colors.

Blog

If you have a new blog, make sure it reflects your new color palette. And don't forget to add your branded profile picture.

Resumé

You may be on the hunt for a new job or looking for a job within the same company, but at a different location. You can add color to your resume. You should not do the entire font in a different color, but it can be very stylish for your name and the header of your resume to have a little color.

Logo

If you have your own company, your logo should be in your own colors.

Phone

We will get into business accessories more in chapter 5. But as a realtor, your phone is practically glued to your hand; you may also want to use it as an opportunity to brand yourself.

Look around your office. Look at all your marketing, and make sure it is consistent in delivering your personal color story.

CHAPTER 5

The Gilded Realtor

We've all been there. The uncomfortable and socially awkward event where the atmosphere is so silent that you can hear a pin drop. Everyone is just looking around at each other with awkward half-smiles and pity looks as if to say, "So you got tricked into being here, too."

It is not only the people that are stiff, but also the event. You have probably also been subjected to what are known as "ice-breakers." These torture devices are used to supposedly break the ice and help people to get comfortable with each other. However, the event organizer ends up acting like she is trying to organize activities for a special needs Gymboree class.

You may have been subjected to any of these ultra-corny devices:

The ice-breaker name badge. This is where you write your name and where you are from on your badge. "Why, you are from Fresno too? Well, should we move-in together since we have so much in common?"

Animal trivia. This is where you go around the room and ask people to disclose their favorite animal or which animal they would like to be. (I told you they treat you like a special needs Gymboree class.)

The facebook profile. This is where if it is your turn to share, you give a rundown of your vital stats. Name, where you are from, how long you have worked for your company, single or married, and kids. Next time you are being forced to do this exercise, you can just invite people to look you up on facebook and pass the questioning over to the next person.

Are you feeling bored yet? I fell asleep on my keyboard just from typing it. There is a better way to start conversations or actually have conversations brought to you.

How? It is really simple, if you know human nature. Humans are attracted to beautiful things. If you surround yourself with beautiful things, people will be attracted to you. No, I'm not asking you to hire the cast of Twilight and have them follow you around—although that is an interesting marketing strategy.

In this chapter, we are going to get started talking about your wardrobe and business accessories.

You might be hesitant to bypass this chapter. You may be thinking, "Is she really going to spend a chapter talking about pearl earrings? No, I am not. I was also going to talk about diamond earrings! Just kidding - sort of. This chapter is about gilding the lily, meaning we are going to increase the attractiveness even more adding fashion and business accessories.

Let me make a case for why this chapter is important. In my research of the Top 250 real estate agents in the country, I learned some very important things about their wardrobe choices (more on this in chapter 10). I learned that the Top 250 realtors did two things: they accessorized better and they included more interesting details in their outfits. In short, they were a lot less blah.

In their professional headshots, the Top 250 Realtors wore items that others did not. Try to fill in the blanks below and see what accessories the successful realtors wore.

64% of the Top 250 Realtors wore a _____ versus only 35% of a random sample of realtors.

56% of the Top 250 Realtors wore a _____ versus only 47% of the random sample of realtors.

Turn to Appendix C to learn the answers to the fill-in the blanks above.

Your wardrobe and business accessories are the quickest ways to get rid of the blahs. So let's get started.

12 Must-Have Accessories

Kudos on making it all the way to Chapter 5. If you have made it this far, then you have already completed the fashion basics list found in Chapter 1 of the book. Now we are going to kick it up a notch by making a list of the must have accessories for a realtor.

YOUR WARDROBE ACCESSORIES
Sunglasses
Investment Bag
Clutch
Hoop Earrings
Bangle Bracelets
Watch
Diamond Stud/CZ Earrings (# 7 Apostle of Style)
Cocktail Ring
Pearl Necklace (# 10 Apostle of Style)
Stationary
Belt
Brooch

To create this list, I thought of the ultimate wardrobe stylist challenge. What if I were only allowed 12 accessories to style a photo shoot? What would I choose? In answer to that challenge, I came up with these 12 items. I think these 12 items are a great start to help you begin to build up your stock pile of accessories.

Sunglasses

As a realtor, you spend a lot of time outside and you spend a lot of time driving. Sunglasses are a must-have. The style of sunglasses will depend on your personal style and the shape of your face.

If you have a square face, then you want sunglasses with slightly rounded edges. It may seem counterintuitive, but the rounded edges will help soften your face.

If you have a round face, then you want sunglasses with a more angularity. Again, it is counterintuitive.

If you have an oval face, then you don't want to get glasses that are wider than the broadest part of your face.

If you have a heart shaped face, then look for sunglasses with a gradient, meaning they are darker at the top then at the bottom. It will help to create balance within your face shape.

Investment Bag

An investment bag is a stylish and classic purse that usually has a fancy designer name and is usually a little pricey. Don't worry—later on in the chapter, I'll give you some ways that you can score an investment bag on a small budget and you won't even have to spend the night with the King of Brunei.

The only decision you have to make is whether you want to get the bag in a basic neutral color such as black, brown, or navy, or whether you want it in a stand-out color such as one of the colors in our personal color palette.

When you are first starting to craft your professional wardrobe, my personal advice is usually to start with the basic neutral colors and then branch out. However, this is your investment bag and you want it to shout, "It's your lucky day to be doing business with this realtor!" So the decision is really up to you. Will you choose a basic or stand-out color?

A brief caveat: Merely being by a designer it does not make it an investment bag. You want something that says, "Pow! I am here." I see plenty of women—and in particular, realtors—who have very expensive bags, but they are not attractive. Just because it says "Coach" or "Louis Vuitton" does not mean it is the bag for you.

Clutch

A clutch is a small evening bag that you can clutch in your hand. This is a must for any evening events, and if you make your choice wisely, it can go with almost every evening outfit you have in your closet.

Hoop Earrings

These are a basic. If you can, get them in both silver and gold so you have options.

Bangle Bracelets

I always love having a few of these on set when I am styling because they are so versatile. Bangle bracelets are a large collection of small bracelets that can be worn together or, if it is too much, you can break them up and only wear a few. These are another great basic. If you can, get them in both silver and gold.

Watch

I love watches. I have been going through a watch phase my entire life. A watch is a great accessory to make you look punctual and dependable. Watches can get pretty expensive, so aim for the most expensive looking watch that is still within your budget.

Diamond/CZ Stud Earrings

These were already discussed in Chapter one, but they are so important that I am including them again here. Remember to fake it until you make it, so if you can't afford real diamonds, then cubic zirconium will do just fine.

Cocktail Ring

This oversized ring adds super-sized style to your look. You can wear this with a work casual outfit or sport it at fancy events.

Pearl Necklace

It's so nice, I named it twice. This item was also discussed in chapter one. Make sure to add this to your outfit repertoire ASAP!

Stationery

So maybe this item is not needed on the set of a photo shoot, but it is an essential item for building up your professional network. This item was also discussed in chapter 4 with regard to applying your color palette to your stationery and thank you cards.

Belt

There are so many things you can do with a belt. You can wear it around dresses, cardigans, and jackets to give you more of an hourglass shape. If I had a nickel for every time a belt has saved me during a photo shoot, I would be a very rich woman. For this reason, belts are very important when you are just starting to build your professional wardrobe because you will only have a few items in your wardrobe. Great belts will help you to wear the same thing a different way and everyone will think that you have a zillion clothes in your closet.

For starting out, I would recommend a belt in each of these colors: black, brown, and red.

Brooch

This is a tiny detail that adds a ton of elegance and class. It is also a way to be a little quirky and show off your personality when you have to be in a very button-down suit. You can have everything from a jeweled flower to a jeweled ladybug (not a real ladybug; PETA, please don't protest this book!).

Your Business Accessories

That is it for your wardrobe accessories, but what about your business accessories? This mainly includes all of your tech gadgets. As a realtor, you are on-the-go a lot more than your average professional and you need to be able to work from anywhere, so you have more gadgets than most.

Your hi-tech accessories include: cell phone, laptop, and iPad/tablet.

Your low-tech accessories include pens, business card case, laptop bag, and tablet case.

The important thing to remember is that your gadgets say something about you. I remember when I was first starting out in my own business and I brought my laptop to a client meeting.

The client laughed and made a joke about how big and clunky my laptop was. I was horrified. I then went out later and purchased the thinnest laptop I could, which was the MacBook Air. As conscious as I was about my appearance and the way that I presented myself, I had completely overlooked my laptop. It also probably created a conflict in the mind of my client because the enormous laptop conflicted with polished and sleek image I presented. Getting the new sleeker laptop not only saved my backside, but is also became a great topic of conversation. People were always asking if they could hold or lift up my laptop, and were amazed at how light it was. In fact, the book you are reading now was typed up on a MacBook Air.

The paragraph above was not written to be an advertisement for Apple, but it did help illustrate a point. You probably don't need to have the fastest, sleekest computer out there, but your laptop should not look like you borrowed it from your 10 year old son who is addicted to video games. It should be just as professional and polished as you are.

Your Cell Phone

Your phone is the backbone of your business. Pick up your phone now. Does it look like the phone of a millionaire real estate agent? Is the screen cracked? Do you have a phone cover on it that makes your phone look like fake plastic kindergarten toy? Do you have a work-appropriate ringtone on your phone, or is it Marvin Gaye's Let's Get It On?

Your cell phone is also another great opportunity for branding. You can get a phone cover that is in your color palette. You can get your company name or your name engraved on your phone.

Some other tips on phone etiquette:

Do you have a professional way to answer your phone that also conveys a marketing message such as, "This is Sheila of Never Enough Realty. How can I help you with your real estate needs?"

Have you instructed your staff/team on the proper way to answer the phone, so that clients receive a consistent client service experience? You can have friends and family call in to test your staff.

If applicable, do you have appropriate hold music?

If applicable, can you have a promotional message included at relevant intervals in your hold music?

Business Card Case

Is she really talking about business cards again? Yes, I am. Actually, I am talking about how you carry your business cards. Now you could just carry a stack of them in your wallet. Or you could be a big girl and get a business card case! There are many stylish options. This is another great opportunity for branding—you can get a business card case in your color palette. You can also get a silver or gold one and have it engraved with your name or company name.

Pens

This item was also discussed in Chapter 4 with regard to your color palette. As a realtor, you often have pens at events and especially at open houses so that potential buyers can fill out their information to be contacted later. These pens are great marketing tools, so they should be branded and in your color palette. If you work for a real estate firm, you many not be able to make any personal choices regarding to your pen. But these are the pens that you give out to other people.

Then there is the style decision of your personal pen. Your personal pen should look expensive. They have great looking options at most office supply stores and most of them are pretty affordable. You do not have to go out and get a $500 Mont Blanc pen, but it should be something nice.

The first reason is that when your clients are signing their documents, you want to have a nice pen to hand them to help make the moment even more special.

Second, people are always asking to borrow a pen to write something down, and you want your pen to say something about you. It also feels really good when someone makes the comment, "Nice pen!"

As your income moves up, you can also upgrade to nicer and nicer pens.

Accessories can make or break an outfit

I repeat, accessories can make or break an outfit. When working on photo shoots I quickly learned that about half of the budget had to go to accessories. Most people would think that the clothes and shoes were the most expensive things, but accessories can be pricey. Most of the time you can get designers and shops to lend the clothing, but for the photo shoot you need so many accessory options that it is ridiculous. When you are starting to build your professional millionaire real estate agent wardrobe, remember to leave room for accessories. As I mentioned, I would spend almost half the budget on accessories. And for shopping, I often will make sure that I have a full day to do nothing but shop for accessories.

On set at the shoot, there will typically be a table or two containing nothing but accessories, and I love accessories. I used to be the Accessories editor for the San Diego Examiner. It was a lot of fun and it was hard to believe that my job was just looking at accessories.

Next time you are at the supermarket and you are in the checkout lane, look at the magazine covers (ignore the alien sightings and Elvis is alive magazines). Look at the outfits on the covers and imagine what they would look like without accessories. The outfits suddenly look dull and don't stand out quite as much.

So I apologize if it seems like I am harping on this point, but as I said, I have been at photo shoots and wished I had a certain ring or a certain pair of earrings because it would have taken the look to another level. I want you to go to another level in your business and career, so that means you need to take accessories seriously.

6 Creative Ways To Use Your Fancy Note Cards

I keep talking about note cards and stationery. You went out and you got the postcards that perfectly match your color palette. You have your fancy pen and you are sitting at your desk going, "Okay, now what?" So here are some tips on ways you can boost your business through the use of fancy snail mail:

- ◊ Send a "nice to meet you" card to everyone who has attended your open house.
- ◊ Send a thank you card after you interview for a job.
- ◊ Send compliments to prospective clients. Notice that someone has a great rose *garden in front of their house. Drop them a note to say, "That is a stunning rose garden in front of your house. There are many buyers out there that would pay a premium for that market. If you ever interested in selling your home, give me a call."
- ◊ After events, send a "nice meeting you" card with your business card inside. I have actually received several calls and invitations for lunches and coffee through this approach.
- ◊ If you are trying to recruit top talent to your team or company, use your note cards to send them congratulations when they make the news or receive awards.
- ◊ Of course, send a thank you card after every closed deal.

If you are worried about writer's cramp and worried about finding the time to write all of these note cards, you do have several options. You can have someone on your team do them for you. They can even sign your signature for you. You can also automate it by using services such as SendOutCards.com. You just upload a list of names and addresses and it will send them out for you. You can even have them send out the cards in your own handwriting. Where there's a will, there's a way!

Your Helpers

It may seem a little inappropriate to talk about your assistants under the chapter about accessories. But they are people that help you to get more done so you can be a more effective realtor. If you have assistants, particularly if you have a personal assistant that follows you around and goes with you to appointments, then this section is really important.

And before we get started, yes I know that people are not things. I know that assistants are not to be treated like underlings. And if you are at the level where you have assistants, then "You" have become a business. You are in the business of "You." Don't look over your shoulder; I am talking to Y-O-U!

You by yourself have become a business, like Madonna or Cher (maybe you can even reach one name status like those divas). Because you are a business, you can enact a dress code, particularly if your assistant is interacting with clients. Businesses have dress codes like McDonald's where they are required to wear uniforms. Other businesses are more relaxed and just require a color scheme like all black which is used at businesses like MAC Cosmetics and P.F. Chang's.

Since you are a business, you can have a dress code as well. It might be a little Suzy-psycho if you asked your team or assistants to dress in your color palette (I mean they might be a completely different season than you). However, it may be appropriate to say,

"When we have new client meetings, I want you to wear all black. At open houses/showings, we all wear (insert color here)." You can also do something truly unique by saying that your team/assistants can wear anything they want, except that one item of clothing must be red to connect to your branding. Then your assistant can decide to wear red one day, wear a red headband the next day, and red shoes the following day. It creates a quirky kind of consistency.

This is not a "must do," but it is an attention to detail that your competition is not thinking about.

6 Creative Ways To Stretch Your Accessories Budget

Check out sites like Etsy. Etsy is a site where local artisans can sell their creations. What the accessories lack in a designer label, they more than make up for in their uniqueness. You can spend hours combining through the interesting accessories on this site.

Browse vintage shops. You can often find classic pieces at a discount and many of the items are designer depending on the vintage shops you go to.

Check out estate sales. There are often really great jewelry pieces at estate sales.

Take advantage of sales. Are earrings buy one, get one half off? That is a great opportunity to get a pair of hoop earrings in silver and another pair in gold.

Spend a day accessory shopping. Accessories are usually an after thought. If you take a day and only shop for accessories, you'll find that you start treating it like regular shopping and you'll start searching out deals.

Go in the teeny-bopper store. The stores at the mall that you think are just for teenagers have great accessories options. Go in there and poke your head around. If you can get past the Justin Bieber music, you might have some great accessory finds.

Think of your accessories like staging a property

In selling a property, you have to strike just the right balance between making the home look extremely neat and clean and making it looked lived in. For example, if you wanted to show the dining room of the home, you could have the dining room bare with only a the table and chairs. Or, you could stage the dining room so that there was a floral centerpiece and place settings with place mats, utensils, plates, and napkins. I think it is fairly obvious which option makes for a better presentation. Your outfit and what you wear are like the empty dining room table. Even if it is a beautiful piece of furniture, it can be improved through the correct use of accessories.

Travel Accessories

For this section, I am specifically talking about airplane travel. As a realtor, you do plenty of travel via car. However, there may be occasions when you have to travel for work, particularly if you attend trainings, conferences, and other events.

Of course, the most important fashion statement you can make while traveling is your luggage. You should get the best luggage you can afford; this is pretty obvious. I've bought discount luggage before, trying to save a buck, and it ended up breaking in a year or two. However, there is a designer piece that I splurged on. I still have this piece of luggage and it is in great shape, and this piece has been dragged over cobblestone roads in multiple European countries. Sometimes the price is an indicator of the quality.

However, there are other travel accessories that you might not think of. Your travel accessories are important because you never know who you are going to sit next to on an airplane. You could be sitting next to someone who is going to help you take your business to the next level, so you don't want to be caught in Uggs and your pajamas.

Other important travel accessories:

Your cosmetics bag: This is important because when traveling, you will often have extremely long days, which means you are going to need to refresh your make-up more often. You want a cosmetic bag that makes a statement when it is sitting on the bathroom counter. If you are the female in the airport bathroom that looks like she is the most prepared, women will approach you and ask if you have a certain something to help them. It is another great way to start conversations.

Your blanket or wrap: It is cold on airplanes. Bring a chic (perhaps cashmere) blanket or stylish wrap so you can look fashionable even while you are bundled up.

Neck pillow: Not a must-have, but a nice-to-have. Keep it stylish.

Ponytail holder and bobby pins: This is a must have if your hair is like mine and refuses to stay in place for long periods of time. A ponytail holder and some bobby pins allow you to pull your hair back in a very chic chignon when you exit the plane.

Passport holder: They are fun and oh so stylish. Why not hearken back to the days of the jet set crowd with a sleek and colorful passport holder. There are so many fun styles.

Folder for travel documents: Being organized with a folder for your travel documents shows you are business-savvy. Show them you are also a fashionista-in-training by carrying your documents in anything other than a plain Jane manila folder. Can you get a pink, red, or leopard print folder?

Conversation Starters And Prospecting Scripts

As I mentioned before, when you start dressing better and start accessorizing, you will begin to have people (men and women) come up to you and compliment you on your outfits and accessories. In fact, with my Style Recipe Cards product, I guarantee 20 compliments in 20 days or you get your money back plus $20 (you can find out more about that by visiting www.StyleRecipeCards.com).

To assist you with this process, here are some scripts to help you prospect while you receive your compliments or inquiries about what you are wearing. You can visit www.MillionaireReaEstateAgentMakeover.com to access printable index cards that you can use to help you memorize some of these scripts.

Conversation Starter #1

Potential Prospect: "I love your earrings!"

You: "Thank you. I was a little self-conscious about wearing them, but I am trying to expand my real estate business and I thought these earrings would help me stand out. What brought you to this event?"

Conversation Starter #2

Potential Prospect: "Oh my gosh! Where did you get your dress?"

You: "I really can't remember right now, but if you love it that much, if you give me your business card I can email you and let you know. I can probably even tell you where to get a better deal on it. Do you have your card with you?"

Conversation Starter #3

Potential Prospect: "That is a great color on you!"

You: "Thank you. You just helped me confirm that I should buy more of this color. Maybe this will become my good luck color and help me to sell more houses. What brought you to this event? I'm sure it wasn't just so you could go around complimenting people on the colors they are wearing…"

Conversation Starters #4

Potential Prospect: "You look great. You always dress so nice?"

You: "Thank you. Well, I have to always look nice for my profession. I'm a realtor. I help people find their dream homes. I am sure you do something equally fascinating. If you don't mind me asking, what do you do?"

A Client's Story

Accessories are so important that sometimes entire photo fashion stories are built around them. This particular fashion story was going to be built around hats. A few years ago a ladylike trend was very popular. It is always in style, but it was hot then. Our model for the shoot did a lot of sexy photo shoots and hosted wet t-shirt contests on the weekend, so we were skeptical if she could pull off ladylike. There was one particular look that was this ladylike trend. There was this gorgeous white skirt suit and I wasn't sure if she was going to be able to pull it off. I was very excited about this outfit and a white flowered hat that looked like something Audrey Hepburn would wear in an old Hollywood movie.

So the first outfit of the day was fine, but then we had to change into the ladylike outfit—this white skirt suit. To help her pull off this look, it was all about the accessories. We had this hat. We had long white gloves that a debutante would wear and simple not sexy high heels. There was very simple pearl jewelry, all very classy.

We posed her on an old Parisian-style couch that had an enormous French painting behind it in a very ornate frame. She pulled off the look; she looked extra classy and very ladylike. Mission accomplished!

I am positive that photo would not have come out great if we had not had the right accessories. Similarly, your accessories are going to either make or break the story you are crafting for your business and your brand. Accessories completely transformed the look of this fashion story and turned an unlikely model into someone who looked like she just left a polo match. Your accessories will do the same thing for you.

I see it happen again and again, both in front of the camera and in real life with real people. The accessories are going to completely transform you so that you can say to yourself, "There. Now I look the part of a Millionaire Real Estate Agent."

Many people can often find accessories more overwhelming than shopping and building a wardrobe because there are so many options available. One of my favorite things is the accessories table at a fashion shoot. It just makes me smile when I see a table spread out with all of the great accessory options that really make a look. Often, once women get a handle on their wardrobe and start dressing better,+- the accessories piece is still lacking and they will think, "How come I don't look as put together as her?" The answer to that question is always the accessories.

Unfortunately, what I see with many image consultants is that they will craft a professional look for someone and get the suits, etc., but they forget the accessories. It is one of the reasons that I chose a degree in fashion styling as opposed to a certificate in image consulting. I wanted to be able to craft an entire character, not just shop for people.

Accessories are tough to nail. I am often working on a job and a model or photographer may be thinking, "I can do that." But once you start to add the accessories on, they begin to see why you are a fashion expert and how someone just going shopping at the mall would not be able to pull off what you do. Luckily, we live in an age where there are a number of tools and resources to help women with this tricky skill. I have created a special no- fail formulas to help women accessorize and look like a pro.

End-Of-Chapter Bonu$:

Here is the killer business application for this chapter. Accessories are conversation starters. People will come up to you and compliment you on your wardrobe accessories and business accessories.

If you want to get someone's attention, send them a gift. If there is a woman at an event that compliments you on your earrings, you can purchase a similar pair and send it to her with a note. Of course, this only works if it is something that is not too pricey and it will depend on how badly you want to get her attention.

This also works great for pens, cell phone covers, business card cases, and other little baubles. But you should look as these gifts as a marketing expense. How much does it cost you to acquire a client through advertising? A $25 pair of earrings seems insignificant if you look at it in that light. I guarantee that very few, if any, of your competitors are doing this sort of thing.

If you can't afford to give a little bauble or someone compliments you on a more expensive item, say your laptop bag, you can always later send them the name or website where you bought the item. Of course, this information will be enclosed in a beautiful note card that also contains your business card.

In addition, when you get referrals from this person, it already puts you in a good light. She will introduce you as, "This is Marie. She bought me these gorgeous earrings. You'll love working with her." Who wouldn't want to work with you after an introduction like that?

CHAPTER 6

The Powerful Realtor

When politicians and captains of industry have to make big speeches, great detail goes into deciding which suit will be worn and, more importantly, which tie will be worn. This special tie is called a power tie because it conveys authority and power. It says "I'm in charge".

As women, we also have a power accessory… it is called the push-up bra. I'm just kidding! This book is not about to take a turn toward Fifty Shades of Gray (try to mask your disappointment). The push-up bra can be an important accessory, but that is not what this chapter is about. This chapter is about the power outfit—how to convey power and authority with just your wardrobe; how to capture a room and send off the vibe of "I'm in charge" or "I will soon be in charge."

Let The Men Have Their Power Ties, We Have Our Power Outfits

Your power outfits are the outfits that you pull out when you need to be "On." You look your best in these outfits, your self-esteem climbs every time you slip one on, and you look fantastic every time a photo is snapped of you in the outfit.

There is a very prominent speaker who refers to these outfits as her "uniforms." They are her uniforms for success. She has three of them and they hang together in her closet. When she has to travel for a speaking engagement, she decides which uniform she wants to bring for the stage. These outfits have been battlefield-tested and are stylist-approved; she looks great and feels great every time she wears them.

She has also successfully reduced the stress level in her professional life. She does not have to worry about going out to find a new outfit. She has three of them right there so she can focus on travel and her speech. Also, when she returns, she takes the entire outfit straight over to the dry cleaners so it can be returned cleaned and pressed to her closet, ready for her next opportunity.

As a wardrobe stylist, I have the added benefit of being extra OCD; I take organizing power outfits to the next level. Each outfit hangs complete on a hanger, with an index card attached that even states which undergarments to bring. For example, this one requires a beige bra, a thong, and black pantyhose. It makes the process even more seamless while the client is getting ready.

In the age of digital photography, I can also include photos of some different ways to accessorize and wear the outfit (I can put these photos on some clients' smartphones for their easy reference). This becomes more important as a client creates a greater reputation for herself and doesn't want all the photos of her to be in the same outfit.

If you want to be a successful realtor, you need to get some power outfits.

Where And When To Break Out The Power Outfit

As a realtor, you have plenty of occasions to wear your power outfits. Think of the times you need to add a little extra "power" to your confidence, such as:

- New client meetings
- Open houses
- Important negotiations
- Job interviews
- Industry events
- Speaking engagements
- Important networking events
- Special events
- Professional head shots and photos
- Important staff meetings

New client meetings - New client meetings are a great time to wear your power outfits. First impressions are your paycheck, and new client meeting are always about first impressions.

Open houses - You are playing hostess and tour guide all rolled into one. An open house is a great time to look professional and detailed-oriented so the home buyers will feel comfortable with you. Your professional "power look" lends credibility to the information you are telling them about the property.

Important negotiations - Negotiations are nothing but power plays. Give a power boost to your power dynamics by wearing your power outfit to key negotiations.

Professional head shots and photos - According to the National Association of Realtors, 85% of home buyers begin their search online. This statistic means that your professional photos are more important than ever. Prospective clients may be judging you by your photo, or worse—your photo is a poor reflection of the properties you are trying to sell. Your professional photo is the best place for your power outfits. Plus, once you start breaking sales records, announcements of your success may end up in the local newspaper or industry publications. You want your photo to scream success.

Job interviews - If you are interviewing for a job, of course you want your confidence at full capacity and you want to make a great first impression. Your power outfit should absolutely be front and center at your next job interview.

Industry events - Don't you want to look like a mover and a shaker when you are around your colleagues at industry events? The power outfit is your way to instantly look like a key player in your industry.

Speaking engagements - Of course when you are on stage, you need to be wearing one of your outfits. You want to be the center of attention because you literally are, as you are on stage giving your speech.

Important networking event - Sometimes you attend an event because you know that someone you want to be introduced to will be there. This is another chance where a first impression can make or break a relationship with a potential client or referral source.

Special Events - Occasionally you get invited to parties, award ceremonies, and other celebrations. The power outfit is a great way to be life of the party by virtue of what you are wearing. Special events are extremely important because they are usually heavily photographed, and today with social media and blogs, you never know where those pictures are going to end up. You don't want someone googling your name and have awful pictures show up at the top of the search results.

Important Staff Meetings - Do you run an entire office or even a team? If so, then you know that there are many occasions where you need to command the attention of your team. Being dressed in your power outfit tells your team that you mean business and that you are a person to be respected. For your next important meeting, dress in your power outfit and see how your staff responds to you.

Elements Of A Great Power Outfit

How do you know if you have a great power outfit on your hands? You know you have a great power outfit if:

- ◊ You receive a ton of compliments every time you wear it
- ◊ It stands out from the crowd
- ◊ The color highlights your eyes and hair color
- ◊ You feel ready to take on the world when you wear it
- ◊ You stand up straighter
- ◊ There are undertones of envy when you are around your coworkers

Create Your Very Own Power Outfit

There are 3 options for your power outfit:
- ◊ A pants suit
- ◊ A skirt suit
- ◊ A dress with a jacket

The three power suit options all include a jacket. You will look more professional with a jacket, so you want to create the outfit with the jacket. There is also the option of removing the jacket if you want a more casual look. Ideally, though, the outfit should include a jacket. In fact, my research has shown that of the women on the list of the Top 250 realtors in country, most are more likely to wear a jacket in their professional photos.

A power outfit pantsuit is a great option; it is oh so Hillary Clinton. Many women prefer to wear pants rather than a skirt (however, if you have great legs flaunt them). The pantsuit says power broker. If it is good enough for the former Secretary of State, then surely it is enough to handle any negotiations you might have to face.

A more feminine option is the skirt suit. It provides the professionalism of a suit, but the femininity of a skirt. A great way to give your wardrobe tons of mileage is to buy a suit and purchase both the skirt and pants of the same suit so you can wear it with either your skirt or your pants.

A less traditional option is the dress with the jacket. Often, these may not have come as a pair and it you just happen upon this great pairing. It is like discovering the perfect wine to go with your cheese platter.

A Radical Idea

I am also going to make another radical suggestion here, departing from traditional fashion advice (hopefully the fashion gods will not smite me). I am going to advise that your power outfit is a color other than black. Yes, black is slimming but you can also look slimming in other dark colors such as:

- ◊ Dark Chocolate Brown
- ◊ Grey
- ◊ Forest Green
- ◊ Deep Red
- ◊ Plum
- ◊ Navy

If you must wear black, then the outfit needs to be perfectly tailored so it fits you like it is a custom-made suit. Tailoring is important for any of your power outfits, but because the suit is black, it does not stand out and the fit becomes that much more important.

Think Of It As An Investment

As they say, it takes money to make money. If you do not already own a power outfit or don't have anything you can convert to a power outfit, then you will need to go out and purchase one. This is something you should spend money on. You should pay more for this than any of your other items. If done correctly, this outfit will pay for itself, and it may be sooner than you think. I know one female entrepreneur who went out and splurged on a designer suit and she went out and had her best month after purchasing the suit. Now, she knew it wasn't the suit that made the sales; it was who she was in the suit. She exuded more confidence and, of course, attracted more success as a result of that.

If there was a place to skimp in your clothing budget, this is not the place. Also, if you spend money getting a better quality suit, then you will wear it for years and years. You need to think about your power outfit as a new laptop or office desk or cell phone. It is something that helps you to be more productive and make you more money.

Is the price tag the only way to know if it is a high quality suit?

No, price is not the only way to tell. With more and more big-name designers slapping their names on clothing designed for the mass market, it is hard to know if you are paying for the quality or if you are paying for the name. There are a couple of things you want to look at when trying to assess the quality of the suit:

A really good suit is going to have nice lining. There are plenty of blazers and dress pants that you can get that do not have a lining in them. If you are going for quality and this is your power outfit, then you want to have items that have a lining.

A really good suit will have nice buttons. You will want to look at the buttons and see if they look like they are made from not so sturdy plastic. Nicer suits will have nicer, sturdier buttons that will last longer.

A good suit will have some weight to it. The heaviness of the fabric will give you a sense of the quality of the fabric used.

A great fit

The shoulders should fit. We are not trying to be Melanie Griffith in a 1980's movie (that was a reference to the film Working Girl for you non-movie fanatics). That means the shoulders on the jacket should not go out past your shoulders. If you stand sideways up against a wall with your shoulder toward the wall, the shoulder pad should not touch the wall before you do. If it does, the jacket is too big. You'll know if a jacket is too small because you will not be able to close it, or you'll be passed out in the dressing room from lack of circulation.

Won't Everyone Get Tired of Seeing Me in the Same Outfit?

By now it should dawning on you that the power suit is very important, and that you can get a little mileage out of it. But you are also probably starting to wonder how you can possibly wear the same outfit over and over and over and over again without people starting to notice. You don't want to become the Where's Waldo of real estate. You attend an event and your colleagues can easily spot you in a crowd, thinking, "Oh, there goes Lisa again in her same red suit."

I had a client who attended an annual event. For the first year, I created an outfit for her (she got rave reviews of course). The next year, she decided to wear the same thing because she got compliments before, so why not? However, she changed her mind at the last minute, and we created a new outfit.

At the event, they had a jumbo slideshow going on—one enormous wall of the conference center. There she was in photos in King Kong proportions wearing her outfit. She was so glad that she decided not to wear the same thing; it would have been embarrassing to be so prominent and wearing the exact same thing.

There are ways to mix up your power outfits so that they look different every time. The key to this strategy is going to be accessories and a few other key pieces which, if you have acquired the 12 Apostles of Style, will be a cinch.

One Suit 7 Ways

You have your power outfit. It is a gray pantsuit that is fitted to perfection. It hugs all the right curves and gracefully lays over the not-so-nice curves. You spent a lot of money on this suit and you need to get the maximum ROI out of this investment. Here are 7 ways you can wear the same pants suit:

- ◊ Wear it as a straight pantsuit with a button-down blouse with a collar. This is the simplest way to sport a suit of this kind. If you want to escalate the style, instead of wearing it with a white blouse, try it with an unexpected color, like a deep purple.

- ◊ Swap out the pants and wear it with your black pencil skirt (the #11 Apostle of Style). The great fit of the jacket will help keep this power outfit super-charged.

- ◊ Wear it with a statement necklace. For example, wear your pantsuit with an emerald green shell/tank top and a complimentary emerald and silver statement necklace. It will look like a completely different outfit

- ◊ Wear your pantsuit with your cashmere turtleneck (the #3 Apostle of Style). This is a great look for winter. You can wear it with a black or cream sweater or go monochromatic and with a complimentary gray color.

- ◊ Go metallic by wearing your suit with a shimmery silver metallic top and matching silver strapped high heels. This is a great look for parties and events. Don't forget your matching clutch.

- ◊ Show some more curves by adding a belt. This won't work on all jacket styles, but try adding a belt around the closed jacket for a more cinched in waist look.
- ◊ Wear the suit with an interesting brooch or group of brooches on your jacket. This little detail can add large amounts of "chicness" to this suit.
- ◊ A touch of red. Wear the suit with a white top, red belt, red shoes, and a red handbag. Classic and oh so magazine-worthy. Take the look over the top with red fingernails and red lipstick.

If you want to see the design boards for these different outfits, visit www.MillionaireRealEstateAgentMakeover.com to access the bonus features.

A trick to even more confidence

The power outfit will definitely give you more confidence, but in the beginning you may need an even bigger boost of confidence. There is a scientifically proven method to increase confidence, and it only takes 2 minutes.

Google the TED talk by social psychologist Amy Cuddy. She explains how power posing can help you in situations where you need to perform. This talk is extremely enlightening and something every woman should hear, because it can help to make you more aggressive, more of a risk-taker, and more of leader. These are all characteristics you can use to be more competitive in the ultra-competitive world of real estate.

Traveling With Your Power Outfits

You might be able to get away with packing your power outfit in a suitcase; however, if you want it to arrive there with fewer wrinkles, you may need to take a cue from the businessmen you see at the airport and invest in a garment bag.

If you have time once you arrive at your location, you may be able to have your outfit sent out to be steamed, but if you don't have enough time, the garment bag is the way to go. I've learned this lesson the hard way by trying to stuff clothing into trunks and boxes for photo shoots.

Now that you are on your way to becoming a millionaire real estate agent, you'll want to have garment bags and luggage that reflect your new status. Spring for a garment bag that is sturdy and just as fabulous as you are.

More Additions To Your Emergency Kit

We are continuing to put together a fashion emergency kit. Now that you have power outfits, there are several more things you need to throw into your fashion emergency kit:

___ Lint brush

___ Wrinkle releaser spray

Lint brush

The lint brush is vital. They now come in many different sizes, including mini ones so they are easy to tuck into numerous places. If you have pets such as dogs and cats, then the lint brush is going to be absolutely essential. While you are at the store, buy a multi-pack; you will be surprised how quickly you will go through it.

Wrinkle releaser spray

This stuff is great. You spray it on and it can reduce the amount of wrinkles in your fabric. It is great for when you don't have access to an iron. After running around all day or driving around in car, your clothes can get quite wrinkled. This is a great way to refresh your clothing.

Power Photo Taking

Now that you have great power outfits, you need to show them off. Attending social and industry events is a great way to network your way into $even figure$. These events also have many, many photo opportunities. See the end-of-chapter bonus to learn how to leverage these photographs into more business.

Before your makeover, you may have been a wallflower. You may have been the person who stood in the back of group photos. Not anymore; you want to be seen! You need to get out of your comfort zone; the success of your business and career may depend on it.

There are two great places in group photos. You either want to be front and center or on either side. It makes for an easier conversation if you can say, "I am the one in red up front" or "I am the one on the right side in pink."

A Client's Story

The power outfit is about having a go-to outfit that you can use when you really need to look your best and feel as confident as possible. The power outfit is also about helping you stand out in a crowd. Imagine being in a crowded room full of people dancing. There are people movin', groovin', and gyrating all around it, and you need to stand out from that group people. Imagine you have to catch everyone's attention and pull focus from all the people around you.

That is exactly the situation you are in when you are working on a music video shoot. This is the time when you need the ultimate power outfit. I was working on a video shoot with a young up-and-coming pop star and we were attempting to shoot 2 videos in one day. It ended up being about a 20 hour day. All the background dancers (girls) had to be dressed really trendy. The director was going for a Gossip Girl/Private School Girl uniform look. It was very trendy at the moment. In fact, that is when I first started watching Gossip Girl, because I had no idea what the team was talking about. The background girls had to be dressed very cute, but not sexy—after all, these were underage teenage girls. However, the singer still had to pop in a room full of well-dressed girls.

There was definitely some fancy footwork done, mixing and matching accessories, trying things on, getting a color that did not blend. It was a lot of work to make her pop and look like America's next pop star. This trick was accomplished by using color. For one scene, we went with a bright purple color. We also used some very unique and on trend accessories of the moment like the fingerless half motorcycle gloves (seen in various fashion shoots and other music videos), and an outrageous jacket in a nighttime scene. Again, it's about knowing the brand, seeing the vision of what the brand can become, and executing it through well-thought-out wardrobe pieces and accessories.

After working on challenging jobs like that, when a realtor asks me to create a power outfit for her I ask, "Do you want me to do it blindfolded with my hands tied behind my back?" That is not a challenge and can be created many ways. Being on a set full of pre-teen and teenage girls with too many outfit changes to comprehend is a real challenge. And it took me at least three months to get that song out of my head! Realtors are a sweet relief to the level of insanity contained within the music industry.

The whole point of creating the power outfit is to have a no-fail formula for creating an outfit that you look great in and feel confident in. When you have very important moments in your career, you want to look great, but you have enough to think about. By doing this work up front, you can wake up, look at calendar, and just know that it is going to have to be a Power Outfit kind of day. You simply go to your closet and get dressed in one of these outfits. No thinking required; you are on auto-pilot, but you look like you have spent hours getting ready because you look so good.

You can do this with your entire wardrobe and achieve this level of style every day. This was the basis of my creating Style Recipe Cards. I wanted people to be auto-pilot chic. Now with power outfits, you use this auto-pilot technique to be a chic, confident, and powerful realtor.

End-of-Chapter Bonu$:

If you have followed the advice in this chapter, you have 2 to 3 power outfits. You've been seen out and about in these outfits and taken dozens of pictures at dozens of events, looking fabulous in every picture. Now, how can you make this work for you even more and multiply your ROI? Here's the strategy:

Make sure you have your camera or camera phone with you at every event you attend.

Make sure that when everyone takes a picture, your camera is in there snapping pictures.

After the picture is snapped, try to get the name or business card of everyone in the photo with you. You can either email or text the photo to yourself and include the names of people in the photo with you. You can also use an app such as Evernote to add notes to your photos.

Once you leave the event, add these photos to your various social media accounts and reach out to people to share photos with them. People are always interested in photos of themselves.

You can also go the low-tech option and print the photos and mail them to the people in the photos if you have their addresses. Make sure to include your business card in the mailing. People will appreciate you taking the time to mail them the photos and it is a great way to bring these people into your potential client or referral circle. Plus, people will have the ultimate business card, you looking great in a photo wearing your power outfit that screams successful real estate agent.

CHAPTER 7

The Photogenic Realtor

I remember being the model in a photo shoot. As we changed locations in the model home and I changed outfits, I remember saying to the photographer, "Don't make my photo look like a 'real estate agent photo'." She laughed and it helped to break the ice. However, the reason that it was funny is because we both perceived realtor photos to be awful.

I guess that was my first encounter with making a link between realtors and style. My second encounter was much more of a "lightening strike." I was sitting at a light, waiting for it to turn red. As I am sitting at the light, I look over and I see a bus bench with a realtor advertisement on it. I looked at the advertisement and wondered, "Why are they all so boring? I would never style someone like that for a photo shoot." Right there, I made the mental leap to, "I am a wardrobe stylist and there are a group of women out there in desperate need of some help!"

I also realized that if I could describe a photo style as "real estate agent," then that is the majority of what is out there in the marketplace. This means that if someone were stylish with great photos, they would drastically stand apart from their competitors. We are not talking about standing out a little—the stylish realtor would be towering over her competition because the industry is full of the plain and mundane, or as we say in fashion... it's vanilla.

After styling several clients, I wondered if there was some link between style and success in the real estate industry. Of course in entertainment, pageants, and other public figures, there is a link. That is why many wardrobe stylists work primarily in those fields.

But I was seeing more and more evidence that there was a link in the rest of the world among every day people.

More of this will be covered in Chapter 10, but for now let's focus on your photo so you don't have a "Real Estate Agent Photo."

Why Is Your Photo Is So Important?

As a realtor, you actually have a lot in common with actresses. One of the most important marketing materials for an actress is her headshot. Her headshot document consists of her photo on the front and her resume on the back. As a realtor, almost all of your marketing materials will feature a photo of yourself. There are not many other professions that have that distinction.

For this reason, a great tip is to find a photographer that does head shots and not one that does "real estate photos." You want to find someone who does head shots, not portraits. Many portrait photographers will make you look like you are taking a photo for the 35th grade!

If you were marketing a property, you would take the best photo possible at an angle that is the most flattering and sets it apart from all the other photos. Most realtors do not pay as much attention to marketing themselves, even though marketing themselves better will lead to being able to list more and better properties.

Your photo also tells something else about you. It can hint at your income bracket. In research that I've conducted, I looked at the Top 250 realtors in the country and analyzed their professional head shots. Their photos were quantifiably different from the photos of the average realtor. There will be more on this in chapter 10, but let's just say that the Top 250 realtors are better at marketing an putting forward a more polished image.

Getting Your Photos From The Photographer

After your photo shoot, your photos will not be available right away. Your photographer is going to want to touch them up. They will also discard any of the photos that are no good—meaning they will toss out any of the photos where your eyes are half-closed or it looks like a hair is sticking up from the side of your head.

This is actually a sign of a good photographer. They will edit the photos before you see them because they only want to show their best work. They will not want bad photos out there with their name associated with them.

From the photographer, you are going to request a CD or thumb drive containing all of the photos. These are high resolution photos, so the file size is very large and if the photographer makes these available on a website, they can sometimes take forever to download simply because they are so large.

You want to have the large, high-resolution photo files because that will cover you for all of the marketing that you will want to do. This will cover you for anything that is to be printed, anything for the web, and anything you might want to have enlarged—for example if you decided to do a billboard or bus bench advertising, or anything else you may think up.

The files types for these photos should be .jpg or .png.

The 20 Questions That Can Change The Outcome Of Your Photo

◊ To the photographer - Can I see your portfolio?

Just like when you hire a contractor for a renovation, you want references and referrals. A photographer's portfolio contains his or her references; you can see exactly how the final product turned out.

◊ To the photographer - Do you do head shots for models, actresses, etc.?

You want a photographer who has experience working with people that need to look good for a living. You don't need to find a photographer that includes Vogue magazine as one of their clients. You will be surprised at how many photographers do head shots for even amateur celebrities, such as the newscasters in your local area. A great source to find these photographers is the website www.ModelMayhem.com

◊ To the photographer - Do you airbrush photos? Can I see before and after examples?

You want a photographer that has some computer skills. Airbrushing is a deal breaker—they must be able to do this, otherwise you can end up looking like a leather muppet when all of your wisdom creases show up in the photograph.

◊ To the photographer - Do you provide a CD with the digital photos?

You want the actual digital photos in a really high resolution such as 300 dpi. The file sizes for this are fairly large. You want high resolution photos because it will allow you greater flexibility. You will be able to use the photos for small print projects and large print projects like bus stop/subway billboards.

◊ To the photographer - Do you allow outfit changes during the photo shoot?

A lot of times a photographer will let you know how many outfit changes they will tolerate. You want to find someone who will let you do 2 to 3 outfit changes. You want to let them know about this ahead of time, because for photographers, time is money. And if the photo shoot takes longer than allotted, they will be "losing money."

◊ To the photographer - What backgrounds do you use?

A lot of photographers will use some sort of gray or dark blue background. You want to make sure to let them know that you need these photos for a variety of marketing materials, so you need at least some of the shots on a white background so it will blend in with the rest of the marketing pieces.

◊ To yourself - Should I hire a beauty team, or do I make individual appointments?

Many times you can hire a beauty team that includes hair and makeup people. These beauty teams do a lot of events like weddings, but they are a lot more hungry for business on weekdays. You may be able to hire them for a more affordable rate. Remember this is an investment; your head shot is just like having a business logo designed. This single image is going to represent you and your business, so you need to make sure it comes out right.

The alternative to hiring a beauty team is to make individual appointments to get your hair and your makeup done on the day of the photo shoot.

For makeup, you can either hire a makeup artist or you can go to a makeup counter to have your makeup done. Usually, if you go got a makeup counter, it is not free—you have to buy a certain amount of makeup in order to get your makeup done. You can use it as an opportunity to stock up on products that may be running low.

◊ To the makeup artist - Can you put on false eyelashes? Do I need to bring my own or do you provide them?

I think false eyelashes are a must for photo shoots, because to me they make your eyes look "normal" in photos. You need to ask your makeup artist about this in advance so he or she can make sure to have them on hand.

◊ To the hairdresser - Can you style my hair so it will last more than 4 hours?

You have to let the hairdresser know that you need your hairstyle to last. They will use more products so that it will hold, and sometimes they may curl your hair but not brush it out. They may curl it and pin it so that you brush out the curls when you arrive at your photo shoot. If you do not tell them this information, you may have a non-hairstyle on your hands halfway through your photo shoot.

◊   To your hairdresser - Can you ad a little extra shine to my hair for the photos?

You want you hair to look like a shampoo commercial. Your hairdresser may spray on some shine spray so that you can be ready for your close-up; the only function of this spray is to make your hair shiny.

◊   To yourself - Can I do my own makeup or do I need a professional?

By now, you should know my answer to this. Get a professional to do your makeup. This applies to most people; however, there are some women that have makeup training. I know someone whose best friend is a makeup artist, so she learned from her best friend how to do makeup for the camera.

I know how to do makeup better than most, but I still prefer to have a professional do it. My friends that are photographers are always asking me to do test shots for their portfolios. I always ask to have a makeup person even if we are doing a very casual shoot, because I want the image to be perfect.

◊   To yourself - Which 3 outfits should I bring to the photo shoot?

You should aim to have 2 to 3 outfit changes at the photo shoot. You should know what the outfits are going to be, as well as know all the accessories that go with each outfit.

Here is a huge tip that I have learned from doing photo shoots. You will have a favorite outfit. You may be tempted to wear that outfit first because you want to wear it when your makeup and hair are fresh. Don't do this. Save it for the 2nd outfit. As the photo shoot progresses, you will loosen up and the photos will come out better when you are more relaxed and comfortable.

◊   To yourself - Do the clothes that I'm bringing need to be cleaned and/or ironed?

Make sure your clothes are clean and wrinkle free. It is not fun when you have to improvise because you suddenly see a stain on an item of clothing.

◊   To yourself - Do I need to do my nails?

Yes. I remember that I was heading to a photo shoot, I was already running behind schedule, but I couldn't skip my nail appointment. My friend with me was like, "Why do you need to get your nails done?" and I remember saying that I need to arrive ready for anything, even though I was told that it was primarily going to be head shots. I arrived at the studio and there was a shot planned where I had to stand behind a chair with my hands on the chair. My nails and my perfect French manicure were perfectly visible. That was the photo that was selected by the photographer. I was so glad that I got my nails done, even though it caused me to arrive on set just in the nick of time.

◊   To yourself - Do I have my happy thoughts that always make me laugh when I think about them?

You are not trying to win America's Next Top Model. Your photo does not need to be fierce. Your photo should be professional and happy. It should be high on the "Know, Like, and Trust" factors that are discussed so frequently in marketing. A potential client should look at your photo and feel like they know you. The photo should make them like you. And the professionalism of the photo should make them trust you.

What I often see happen is that real estate agents will look at what other people are doing in their industry and copy it. It's just a mindset of, "Well, this is what everyone else is doing." There is not a marketing or branding approach taken to the photo. So to create the "Know, Like and Trust" factors, you need to appear happy in your photo. Since very few realtors are Oscar winning actresses (try to name one), you won't be able to fake it. You will need your Happy Thoughts. Think of things that make you laugh or smile.

You can think about your kids and your partner and those things might make you smile, but I want you to think of things that really make you happy. Think of jokes that always make you laugh, like scenes in movies or TV shows. Use these Happy Thoughts during your photo shoot and the happiness will twinkle in your eyes.

◊ To yourself - Do I need to whiten my teeth before my photo shoot?

Only if you think you need it. If you are going to whiten your teeth, I would do it a few weeks before the actual photo shoot. Depending on the method you use, it can take a few weeks before you see full results.

◊ To yourself - Do I need to purchase a body shaper?

Again, this is a personal decision. Not everyone needs one, but sometimes people wear it just because it helps them to feel less self-conscious. You may be intending to go in and only get head shots, but you should be prepared in case they also take full body photos.

You can always purchase the body shaper; you can try it on with your planned outfits. If you don't need it, you can always return it. My experience has been, once you try on clothes with a body shaper you'll want to wear it. If it is your first time, you will gaze in wonderment at your body and be asking if you can buy stock in Spanx.

◊ To yourself - Do I have all the accessories I need for my outfits?

You are not a wardrobe stylist, so you will not arrive at the shoot with a table full of accessories; you need to pick yours out in advance. Gather up all your accessories, place them in a small bag and bring it with you to the shoot.

◊ To yourself - Are all of my outfits in my color palette?

You made it all the way to chapter 6, so this should be a "No, duh!" by now. The purpose of the photo is that to be the cornerstone of your marketing. Your photo obviously needs to be branded with your personal color palette.

◊   To yourself - Did I practice in front of a mirror?

Warning: This is going to be very uncomfortable. You are going to feel like you are in the running for the title, "World's Biggest Narcissist." However, this really works and it really helps. You want to practice your poses and your faces in the mirror. Make your mistakes here, while you are not paying a photographer. You don't want all your hard work to be a waste because you didn't practice. It doesn't take long, and you can practice in the morning when you are already looking in a mirror to get ready for work.

Countdown To Photo Shoot

Book a date for your photo shoot. The further away you make the appointment, the more flexibility you will have for your other appointments.

- ◊   The same day you book the photographer
    - ◊   Book your hair and makeup appointments.
- ◊   Three weeks before photo shoot
    - ◊   Get your teeth whitened, if applicable.
- ◊   Two weeks before photo shoot
    - ◊   Go shopping for your photo shoot outfits in your closet.
    - ◊   If you don't have outfits, go shopping to buy outfits for photo shoot.
- ◊   One Week before photo shoot
    - ◊   Get your happy thoughts.
    - ◊   Start practicing in the mirror.

- ◊ Go shopping for undergarments/body shapers, if applicable.
- ◊ Buy false eyelashes, if applicable; makeup artist may be supplying them.
- ◊ Try on items with and without body shaper.

◊ Three days before your photo shoot

- ◊ If you wax, get any waxing done that you need. This isn't a shoot for Sports Illustrated, so you can skip the bikini wax. However, you may need to wax any facial hair, arm pits, or legs.

◊ Two days before your photo shoot

- ◊ Start drinking more water.
- ◊ Avoid salty foods.
- ◊ Avoid alcohol.
- ◊ All of the items above will help prevent puffiness the day of your photo shoot.

◊ The day before your photo shoot

- ◊ Iron and prep your clothes.
- ◊ Shape your eyebrows.
- ◊ Have your clothes and accessories bagged up for easy transport to photo shoot.
- ◊ Get some sleep.

◊ The day of the photo shoot

- ◊ Read the End of Chapter Bonus and work the plan.

◊ The day after the photo shoot

- ◊ Send thank you's to everyone who helped you with the shoot. Read the End of Chapter Bonus and work the plan.

Aisha Jones

Let's Go Shopping

The first place to go shopping is your very own closet. You are going to look for colors that are in your color palette that you created in chapter 4.

Before you just blindly go shopping, you should have an idea of the look you are going for. Think about this when you go to the hairdresser and you bring in hairstyle ideas. You can also clip pictures of outfits that you like to come up with ideas for what to buy. This is why people hire wardrobe stylists—they can quickly come up with great ideas and after getting to know your brand, coloring, and body type; they will immediately know what they want to do. This process is really too lengthy to get into now in this book, but it does really drive the overall brand you are trying to create.

The next step is to have an idea of the colors you are looking for. You already developed your personal color palette; you should get some outfits that are in those colors so that they will match your marketing materials.

Before you spend any cash, go to your closet and shop there first. You might find hidden treasures that will make this process easier on your time and your budget. Look for items that are in your color palette and that fit the clippings you have collected.

Next, it is time to really go shopping. I generally like going shopping in areas where I can reach a lot of stores in a short period of time. A lot of times, that ends up being the mall; however, many downtown areas have boutiques all in a row that are a great place to go shopping as well.

Next you have to remember to try everything on because—yes—it looks different on your body than on the hanger. Even though you hate trying things, on it saves you money so you will not have items that you never wear sitting in the back of your closet. It also saves you time and gas money, because you will not have to go back and return items that look horrible on you. I hate trying things on, too, but I don't have a lot of time and I have found that it is a lot more efficient to just head to the dressing room.

Save all of your receipts; you may not end up wearing everything, so you will want to return things. I usually will keep all the receipts in a separate envelope all together.

And that is how you go shopping for your photo shoot.

If your closet has nothing photo shoot worthy, then you have to go out shopping to find pieces that will reinforce your color palette. Shopping will be easy because when you walk into a store, you can focus only on certain colors.

Shopping List

___ 2 to 3 outfits

___ accessories for your outfits

___ body shaper, if applicable

___ false eyelashes, if applicable

How Not To Look Dated In Your Photo

Have you opted to do hair and makeup yourself? In the research that I have performed on the real estate industry and real estate agents, one of the problems I have frequently seen is that real estate agents have photos that look dated. If you are in the industry, you have seen these photos as well. You see some photos that look like they are high school photos from the 80's or 90's complete with feathered hair, gigantic bangs, and/or gigantic hair that is held in place by an unbelievable amount of Aquanet.

How long have you had the exact same hairstyle? Is it still in style? Do you see other successful and stylish people sporting this look?

Are you still doing your makeup the same way? Are you still using the blue eyeshadow that you wore to your senior prom?

A photo shoot is a great reason to re-invent yourself and launch a new brand.

This Is The Brand New You - Get Ready To Face The World

Even though you may have been taking steps to upgrade your appearance and your wardrobe, this new photo is the official launch of the new you. It is launching you as a major public figure, and you must be ready to face the world.

There may be mixed reactions to your new look. There will be some people who love it. There may be other people who hate it. And there will be other people who will be downright snarky in a passive-aggressive way. The thing you can be certain about is that people will have opinions.

One of the things you must remember is consistency. The second wealthiest man in the U.S., Warren Buffet, has said that one of the keys to his success is emotional stability. When the market is up, he is the same. When the market is down, he is the same. He is able to achieve this stability because he is confident of his interpretation of facts and he returns to that again and again, so it does not matter what other people are saying. He did his homework and he is confident.

You need to be confident about your decision to upgrade your appearance and improve your business, and you need to remain consistent more than ever after you have a great photo that is plastered all over your marketing materials. That means every day, you have to put in the effort to look great and look like a successful real estate agent.

You must be conscious of your appearance every day, because you must maintain brand consistency. Your prospects should not meet you and think, "She looks nothing like her picture." If you go to a McDonald's in Maui, is the McDonald's spelled in blue and purple letters? Does a Big Mac in Maui taste different from a Big Mac in Manhattan? Of course not; it is the same. The McDonald's corporation knows how important brand consistency is and they want their customers to know what to expect every time they eat at McDonald's. Similarly, you never want to disappoint your customers and clients; you want them to all have a great experience with you.

To get to Millionaire status, you will have to work harder than ever before and look great while doing it.

A Client's Story

Weddings can be stressful even if you aren't the bride. When we are invited to a wedding, there is often a little stress about what to wear. In fact, the most popular articles I have online are about what to wear to different types of weddings.

I had someone who was the mother of the groom and she needed outfits for the wedding and the rehearsal dinner. I have learned over time that doing my work is much more efficient with the internet. Very often, I don't even have to meet someone and spend a day out shopping. I usually do it online and send the outfits over to them with links on where to buy them. (It is a lot more cost-efficient and allows me to work with a lot of different people.)

So that is what I did in this case. I put together boards of the outfits and sent them to the client. She liked the two dresses, but she had gone to a department store and found another outfit she fell in love with. She decided to use my wedding outfit for the rehearsal dinner and wear the dress she found on her own to the wedding. She sent me a picture of the dress she wanted, and I told her that my dress options would probably be more flattering for her body. She still decided to wear the dress she chose to the wedding.

Well, you probably know how this story ends. The pictures came back from the rehearsal dinner and she looked great. She got the pictures back from the wedding and wasn't so happy. She said she couldn't believe how big her stomach looked. For the next 6 months, she was saying she had to go on a diet because she couldn't believe what her stomach looked like in that dress (like many of us, she never went on the diet).

Although, I never mentioned it to her, my dress would have disguised her belly. I specifically chose a dress with a certain cut and certain detailing to achieve that objective. Her pictures came out somewhat less than flattering. It is unfortunate. It was a happy occasion, but she was reluctant to share the pictures with other people because she did not like how she looked.

In this situation, there is more at stake than just professional headshots. These are photos you want to keep forever and share. These are family memories and they are tucked away.

There are people, tools, and other resources available to prevent these "photo shame" moments from happening to you. As a realtor, you are your brand, so you are your marketing. You don't want to have "marketing shame."

End-of-Chapter Bonu$:

You've finished your photo shoot; now what? Well, before you begin plastering your photo on everything to market yourself, you may want to leverage the contacts that you have just gained from going through the photo shoot process. They can prove to be very valuable contacts and help you to further expand your network and build your business.

Once you have finished your photo shoot, the photographer may ask if they can use your photo for their portfolio or for a sample of their work. This is the passive approach. It's great if this happens, but it always better to be proactive.

For a more proactive approach, you simply ask photographers if they would like their name credited for the photo on your website. They will, of course, say yes. Then you can ask them if they would have your photo in the samples of their portfolio on their site. Ask them to make sure to include your name and company name. A lot of them will be interested because they would probably like to have more professional clients. Exchanging web links with them not only helps you get your name out there, but also helps to boost your search engine search results by creating more links to your website.

Once you come out with a sizzlin' head shot, everyone will be asking you who took your photo. Be generous and send them to your photographer. You can also shoot the photographer an email to advise every time you send him/her a referral. Your photographer should also be on your Christmas card list.

You will want to repeat this process with your hairdresser and make-up artist, if you used them for your photo shoot. This will greatly expand your network with very influential people. Photographers, hair dressers, and professional make-up artists interact with important groups of people for you. They interact with people in higher income brackets, who generally require professional make-up and professional photos.

CHAPTER 8

The Confident Realtor

This is by far the most personal chapter in this book. It deals with confidence. Before we tackle this topic, I think it is only fair to disclose my own struggles with self-esteem and confidence.

As a little girl, I don't remember ever really feeling pretty. I remember relatives and other people calling me pretty and beautiful, but I never really believed them. I always felt that I wasn't "the pretty one;" I was the smart one. In the "real world," smart and pretty didn't go together. If I was smart, then it must mean I wasn't pretty. In all the cartoons, the smart ones wore glasses (which I did starting in the fourth grade). I was very clearly in the smart column.

I was always obsessed with clothes and makeup and beauty. In hindsight, I realize that it probably hinted at what my career should be or what my life's purpose is. At the time, though, I thought the obsession was because I wanted to figure out a process to become beautiful.

I remember that I used to tear out pictures from magazines. I remember there was this one ad for a hair product and I would sleep with it under my pillow and tell God that I wanted to wake up with hair like the woman in the ad. Every night I would make the same wish to God and every morning I would wake up disappointed.

Like most young girls, my self-esteem issues worsened when I hit adolescence. At night, I would stand in front of a mirror and list all the things I wanted to change about myself—my nose, my teeth, this mark on my cheek, my hairline, my eyebrows. It was basically everything about me. As I am writing this, it is bringing back all of those feelings. Standing in front of the mirror in the near dark when I am supposed to be in bed, but instead I am counting off my flaws.

I would brush my teeth and get ready in the morning without looking at myself. I didn't want to look at myself in the mirror because it would start the recitation of the list of flaws--my nose, my teeth, this mark on my cheek, etc...

It got so bad that I did not even want to go out in public. I remember not wanting to go to my brother's basketball game because I didn't want people to see me. I was a hideous monster that would distract from the game. I threw a fit in the parking lot with tears and all because I did not want people to see my ugly face. Once my mom saw this display of tears and heard my reasons, she realized that I needed professional help.

I was in middle school when I first went to visit a therapist. I remember citing off this list to her--my nose, my teeth, this mark on my cheek... oh yeah, and I thought I was fat (I think we all have a little of that and now we wish we could be "fat" like that again).

I worked through a lot of stuff with her. My self-esteem improved, but it was always a constant struggle. Even now, I have to remind myself that looking at myself in the mirror it is okay.

I came out of my shell. I even competed in a beauty pageant and won! When I left for college, my self-esteem was not perfect, but it was a lot better than it had been before.

In college, I met a boy and we eventually got married. If you don't love yourself, if you don't think you are awesome, you surround yourself with people who help prove that you are right. I married someone that helped re-enforce my lack of specialness, my unworthiness, and the fact that I was still only in the "smart" column.

I remember that in pre-marital counseling, the counselor said to him "Your wife is very beautiful. Do you ever tell her that?" He never did. He never called me beautiful or pretty. Even with that revelation in pre-marital counseling, I went ahead with the wedding.

We can fast-forward to three years later, me sitting in my makeshift home office after he berated me about something. I remember an inner voice saying, "I deserve better than this," and I left him and filed for divorce. From the girl who couldn't even look at her reflection in the mirror to having the strength to say "I deserve better than this," that was a victory.

Am I completely cured? Do I have perfect self-esteem and confidence 100% off the time? No way! But I am a lot better.

My marriage was a gift that allowed me to discover who I really am. It allowed me to conquer a lot of my self-worth demons. Without that, I would still be toiling away in Corporate America. I would not have my own business helping women to bring beauty into their lives, and I would not be writing this book.

It is important for me to tell this story because I don't want you to think that I am any different from you. I want you to know that I am not saying this stuff from an ivory tower somewhere. I have been in the trenches and I have helped other people up from the trenches.

In some of my other marketing materials, I mention my friend Corey. Corey was my co-worker back in the day. She was middle-aged, overweight, and married to an alcoholic. Not the have-a-glass-of-wine-after-dinner kind of alcoholic (if you call that an alcoholic); he was the drink-until-you-pass-out-every-night, multiple DUI kind of alcoholic. She was afraid that he was jeopardizing his health, his job, and the financial wellbeing of their family.

When a friend asks you, "Should I leave him?", that is not the kind of question you can answer because your response to that question could change the trajectory of that entire family, so I did what any good friend would do... I took her shopping.

She had a trip out of town to visit her family and she needed some new clothes. I did what I do on any shopping trip with someone—I tell them to go stand in a dressing room and I will bring clothes and outfits to them.

She was a little reluctant to tell me her size, but was surprised when I didn't blink when she said size 22 and was even more surprised that I felt at home shopping in Lane Bryant. As far as I am concerned, style is style no matter your size. She walked out of there with some great pieces. She went on her trip, had a great time, and even got some compliments on her outfits.

We went on a couple more shopping excursions. Corey was dressing better and she was becoming more confident and even sassier. A few months later, she made the decision to leave her husband for the good of herself and her children. So what is the moral of the story?

Leave your husbands…just kidding. It is unfortunate that there are two stories in a row with the same conclusion. There are some really awesome guys out there (I may or may not be dating one of them at the moment, but I don't like to kiss and tell).

The real moral of the story is to get that confidence up as soon as possible, because then you'll soar. So this chapter is dedicated to fun, smart, sassy, and diva-licious exercises you can do to get that confidence up and become a Millionaire Real Estate Agent.

Do you remember the formula? Look Better = Feel Confident = More Sales. If you have done the other personal makeover and business makeover steps in the book, your confidence is already up; now let's kick it into overdrive.

I'm Seeing Red

Red is a powerful color. Red roses mean love, courage, and passion. A red piece of fabric can incite a bull to charge (okay, it's the motion of the fabric, not the color, but that red color was chosen for a reason), and red hair will have you labeled a fire cracker. There is nothing subtle about the color red. You can't hide in red.

Red is my go-to trick when working on a photo shoot, a photo doesn't look quite right or an outfit is not popping in the scene. My crutch is the color red. It works every time, in fact I have to struggle not to constantly choose that when trying to make something work.

Red is so powerful that there is a song and a movie about a woman in red. There is "The Woman in Red" written in 1984 by the great musical genius Stevie Wonder, and then there is the movie by the same name staring Gene Wilder and Kelly LeBrock as the woman in red.

You see your fellow realtor in red and you think she just exudes confidence. This isn't me just blowing smoke up your bum; there is actual research to support this. Studies have suggested that wearing red can inspire confidence in the people who wear the color, and it also has the ability to make opponents quake in the knees. Studies have also suggested that teams that wear red have a greater chance of winning.

Your mission, should you choose to accept it, is to wear red—or more accurately, to wear red lipstick. Not only does it say, "Pay attention to me and what I am saying," but it also has a hint of sex-appeal.

For some of you, this may not be a big confidence challenge, but for me it was huge. I was always made fun of for my lips, so I always just wore lip glosses. No need to bring attention to my lips. I had to wear red lipstick a few times for photo shoots, but in real life, no way.

Then one day I was attending a black tie event, and I decided to wear red lipstick with my outfit. Not just a matte red; it was corvette shiny almost-looked-wet red. It was a huge hit. I still felt uncomfortable in it, but all the photos came out great.

Now on more everyday occasions, I break out the red. My favorite is when I wear an all white outfit with red shiny lips.

Your challenge assignment is to wear red lipstick for a full day. It must be on a day that you will be out working out in the field with clients, not a day where you are at home or at the office working the phone and emails. It is even better if you do it on a day you have an open house or a client walk-through scheduled.

Here are the questions you need to answer after the red lipstick exercise:

- ◊ What brand and what shade of lipstick did you wear?
- ◊ How did you feel when you first put it on? Were you self-conscious? Over-enunciating words?
- ◊ Did people respond to you differently today? If so, how?
- ◊ Did you carry yourself differently today? If, so how?

Remember, if you go to the website and grab the confidence challenge worksheet, fill it out and email it to info@aishajones.com, you will receive a free gift. This is only for the people that complete the challenge, answer the questions and send the worksheet in.

The Compliment Game

The comedian Chris Rock has a famous joke. He says that women need 3 things: Food, Water, and Compliments. There is some truth to that joke, as there is with most jokes. We love to receive compliments and yet many of us do not know HOW to receive compliments.

Many of us will receive a compliment like "Cheryl, I really like your blouse." And then we go, "This old thing? I've had it for ages, and it doesn't really go with this skirt."

You've taken a compliment and deflected it. It is almost as if you can't stand for someone to say something nice about you or to you, so you downplay or make a joke of it, or you say, "Yeah, but still..." Those are not the words and actions of a confident woman and a Millionaire Real Estate Agent.

You should learn to accept a compliment graciously. That means that you say, "Thank You," and return a compliment if it is appropriate.

If you are not used to doing it, then this is going to be hard. Just say thank you and make your mouth stay closed after you say thank you.

If you are going through this makeover process, you are going to get more compliments as you get more polished looking. Your family, friends, and co-workers are all going to start complimenting you more. As you implement some of these business ideas, you will get more compliments from your boss and clients.

I want you to be able to take in all of those compliments and build up your confidence.

So are you ready for your challenge assignment? You have to give out 10 compliments today (your cat Thomas does not count). These compliments could be to your family, coworkers, clients, or the stranger behind you in the supermarket line.

You will be giving out the compliments because a few people will offer you a compliment in return, so you will get to practice accepting a compliment graciously. But, I also want you to notice how people respond to a compliment. Are they responding graciously? Are they deflecting? Are they making a joke out of it?

Here are the questions you need to answer for the compliment game exercise:

- ◊ Who were the 10 people you gave compliments to?
- ◊ Did you recognize your former self in some of the responses you received to your compliments? Were people deflected, downplaying, laughing?
- ◊ Did you receive any compliments back? Did you accept compliments graciously?
- ◊ Do you now think you are worthy of compliments?

Remember, if you go to the website and grab the confidence challenge worksheet fill it out and email it to info@aishajones.com, you will receive a free gift. This is only for the people that complete the challenge, answer the questions and send the worksheet in. You will definitely want this free gift.

Yes, I'm A Diva

This is one of my favorite exercises. The word "diva" has become synonymous with the word bitch. When we hear the word diva, we think of out of control women demanding to be treated like royalty and wanting everyone to act as if the world revolves around them. This kind of personality is frowned upon... a woman who knows what she wants and how she wants to be treated? Good heavens! Next, women will be demanding to be president!

This is contrary to what most of us are taught: be well behaved, quiet, and do what you are told. So because of that well-intended early instruction, many of us are people pleasers and perfectionists. We try to be everything that everyone wants us to be. Our worst nightmare is to be called the "B" word, and you would hate to have the nickname "Diva of Real Estate." However, the "B" gets stuff done. The Diva of Real Estate has clients who are overjoyed because she gets them the best deals and exactly what they want.

I realize that there are extremes at both ends of the spectrum. There is the woman that is the doormat and the martyr who never stands up for herself or her clients, and then there is the Super Diva who throws a tantrum if there are any other colors besides blue M&M's in her candy bowl.

Ideally, you would want to be in the middle between these two extremes. Unfortunately, most women are closer to the doormat end of the spectrum. But to be an effective businesswoman and realtor, you need to have a little diva in you.

Your challenge assignment for this exercise is to act like a diva for a day. As soon as I said that, many of you probably became uncomfortable. That is good. If you want to be successful, you have to get out of your comfort zone. You've already done that by picking up this book, so just take a few more steps outside of that comfort zone.

What do I mean by being a diva for a day... I mean speaking up and asking for what you want. Good is not good enough; you seek perfection today and you expect the royal treatment. Here are some ideas for your "diva attitude" challenge assignment:

- ◊ Have someone help you carry your groceries out to the car. Most of the time we turn down this service, but not on Diva Day.
- ◊ If you go out to a restaurant and the food that comes is not exactly what you want, send it back.
- ◊ If you go to Starbucks, order something difficult and request a specific temperature for your drink. Order something like a Triple, Venti, Half-Sweet, Non-Fat, Caramel Macchiato at exactly 170°.
- ◊ If you get your car washed, have them touch up little spots until the car is perfect and the way you want it.
- ◊ Don't fake an orgasm on Diva Day. If it's not happening, it's not happening.
- ◊ Go shoe shopping and ask the salesperson to bring out at least 10 different types of shoes.
- ◊ Pick up your dry cleaning and inspect it for imperfections. Send it back if it's not perfect.
- ◊ Have your assistant prepare your expense report such that it looks so nice, pretty, and neat that it would make Martha Stewart's head explode.
- ◊ Drink champagne with your breakfast.

- Take a long luxurious bubble bath and pour perfume in it, Marilyn Monroe Style.
- Wear your diamond earrings in the bathtub (be careful with this one).

Think of all of the Diva possibilities. You'll also learn that the Earth will continue rotating and the sun will continue to rise if you say the word "no" or ask for what you really want.

Here are the questions you need to answer for the Diva Day exercise:

- What Diva activities did you do today?
- How did it feel to be a Diva?
- Are there any of the Diva behaviors or activities you want to continue to do even when it isn't Diva Day?

Remember, if you go to the website and grab the confidence challenge worksheet, fill it out and email it to info@aishajones.com, you will receive a free gift. This is only for the people that complete the challenge, answer the questions and send the worksheet in. You will definitely want this free gift.

Miss Universe

When you think beauty pageant, I am sure that the first thing you think about is the bathing suit competition and evening gowns. There is a lot more to beauty pageants than beauty.

If you have ever watched the Miss Universe pageant, you know that in the first five minutes of the competition, they narrow down the finalists to 10 people. As an audience member, you might be thinking the girls only did an opening number and said their names—how could the judges narrow it down to 10 just from that?

Well, in fact, each contestant has had an interview session with the group of judges. Think of this as the worst job interview ever.

You are surrounded by judges and they are throwing questions at you and you have to be poised and confident when you answer them. Oh yeah, they are also judging you on your appearance at the same time. You have to be poised, confident, brilliant, and drop-dead gorgeous... talk about pressure.

The judges are also looking at how you carry yourself when you walk into a room or exit a room. You also have to be more graceful than a ballerina in the way that you move.

If that torture chamber isn't enough, you also have to answer a question on stage in front of millions of people. You probably have new respect for these ladies now. They have to be the complete package. Here are just a few accomplished women, who got their start in pageants:

Oprah Winfrey
Sarah Palin
Delta Burke
Vanessa Williams
Sharon Stone
Diane Sawyer
Halle Berry
Debra Messing
Eva Longoria
Lucy Lawless

Don't worry; this exercise is not going to require you to enter a beauty pageant. But it is going to have you practice your speaking skills and especially your pitch, so you are more confident and so charming that you snag any potential client that comes within three feet of you.

The National Association of Realtors gives potential buyers and sellers 12 questions to ask before they hire a realtor. These are the answers that you need to practice, but you need to do more than practice them. You need to record yourself practicing them.

Yes, for this exercise to work properly you need to watch a video recording of yourself. It could be worse—you could have to watch a porn of yourself. I promise this will do a lot less damage to your psyche.

Here are the 12 questions you need to answer as listed on the National Association of Realtors website:

- How long have you been in residential real estate sales? Is it your full-time job?
- What designations do you hold?
- How many homes did you and your real estate brokerage firm sell last year?
- How many days did it take you to sell the average home?
- How close to the initial asking prices of the homes you sold were the final sale prices?
- What types of specific marketing systems and approaches will you use to sell my home?
- Will you represent me exclusively, or will you represent both the buyer and the seller in the transaction?
- Can you recommend service providers who can help me obtain a mortgage, make home repairs, and help with other things I need done?
- What type of support and supervision does your brokerage office provide to you?
- What's your business philosophy?
- How will you keep me informed about the progress of my transaction? How frequently?
- Could you please give me the names and phone numbers of your three most recent clients?

Number 10 is the question that really helps you sell yourself. This is your pitch. If I wake you up in the dead of night and ask you your business philosophy, you should be able to answer this with your eyes still closed and in the middle of a REM cycle.

I know that initially this may seem silly, but that is how pageant contestants get so poised and confident. They practice, practice, practice. I remember practicing non-stop in my short lived pageant "career" (nothing major, just local pageants). You may also remember the scenes in the movie Miss Congeniality where Sandra Bullock is being drilled endlessly by her pageant coach.

I then translated these same skills to when I have a media event. I recently had to go strut my stuff and show off my Style Recipe Cards on a local TV program. I practiced, practiced, practiced. After our segment finished taping, the host turned to me and said you have your pitch down cold. I did, because I needed to be able to say it with confidence even when I was nervous and even with cameras rolling. Practicing made me feel more confident and look even more confident than I felt.

So there's your assignment. Get out your web cam and record yourself as you answer these questions... and even though this is called the Miss Universe exercise, you cannot answer "World Peace" to any of the questions.

Here are the off-camera questions you need to answer for the Miss Universe exercise:

◊ Did you discover something about yourself in answering these questions?

◊ Did you find a nervous habit or tick that you use when speaking? (I remember my pageant director getting on us about saying "Umm..." Do you do that?)

◊ On a scale of 1 to 10, how bad was it to watch yourself on video?

A Client's Story

One of the scariest things you do as a successful businesswoman or business owner is attend professional events where you don't know anyone. Usually this takes the form of networking events, but sometimes it can even be conferences that take you across the country.

So what do you do if you have an important conference across the country and it is absolutely paramount that you network and make a splash? You call in a wardrobe stylist, of course, and that is exactly what this client did.

This particular event was a multi-day event that included business dinners and breakfasts and a cocktail party.

This particular client was launching a new arm of her business, and was excited to network and tell everyone about it.

The thing that many people don't know is how celebrities use stylists. Let's say that movie star Jane Doe has a new movie coming out, so she needs to a media tour and junkets. A stylist will go and pick out all her clothes (some from shops and some from designers) and make them into outfits. You will usually lay out the outfits and then take pictures, so the celebrity knows that on day 1, this is the outfit you'll wear... sometimes you even have to get specific and say, "Wear this bra so that it doesn't show with this top." Then everything is packed up so the celeb or celeb's assistant can carry everything around with her on her tour. When she sits down for an interview on a Morning Show, then does an interview for an Entertainment TV show, she looks great in all the photos (and never repeats an outfit). This is how stylists also work with professional speakers, celebrity business executives, politicians, authors on book tours, etc...

For this businesswoman's trip, this is what she wanted. She wanted an outfit planned for every single day and every event during her trip. I ordered clothing items ahead of time and arranged them into outfits, and took the pictures so she had a copy on her phone. There was one item she was hesitant about—it was flashy. It was a sequined jacket. Given the theme of the cocktail party (Diamonds and Denim), this jacket was perfect. She didn't know if she had the confidence to pull it off.

I assured her that this jacket was how she would make a splash. I knew that this outfit would single-handedly make her the hit of the party and you know what? I was right? (Of course I was right! if I'd been wrong, do you think I would be telling this story?)

She wore the jacket and she was invited into the VIP area of the party. When she tried to shy away and try to blend into the wall, people shouted, "You can't be shy with a jacket like that on," and they would invite her over to their group. People came up to her all night and complimented her on that jacket.

For the remainder of the conference, she had a great ice breaker to start conversations. People kept saying, "You were the girl with the jacket!" She was still getting compliments days later at the conference.

With the other items I put together for her, people were asking her if she was in the fashion business. They kept complimenting her on her outfits. This turned out to be a very effective and lucrative business trip for her. She made contacts that enabled her to launch another area of her business that now generates about 20% of her income.

I love these types of style stories. This comes down to confidence. This client had to first feel confident enough to realize, "Hey, I need some help with my appearance. I deserve to look great at this event. It will be great for me and my business."

She then had to have the confidence to actually wear the items selected. I'm telling you, I had to really sell her on this jacket. Now she is so glad she wore it. She also has these great pictures of herself in a fabulous jacket with industry bigwigs. These are great photos to put on her business social media sites and to display in her office.

It shows she travels in the same circles as some very important people. That is publicity she couldn't buy. It's priceless. All it cost was the confidence to put on a stylish jacket.

Fashion can make a difference.

This step is so important, because even through you change the outside, you also need to change the inside. You look like a Millionaire Real Estate Agent and now you need to start acting like one. There are many different ways within a makeover process to infuse a little new thinking and new behaviors to make the transformation complete.

End Of Chapter Bonu$:

This end of chapter bonus is a great confidence builder and a great business builder. It gets you talking to people and talking about your business. Remember the pitch you have down cold? Well, now you get to use it over and over again in the 21-day challenge.

For 21 days, you have to talk to 21 new people each day about your business. This could be striking up a conversation with someone in the Starbucks line or connecting with someone on LinkedIn or Facebook. It could even be sending out an email to the stack of business cards that you have on your desk, but you need to connect with 21 people, for 21 days straight.

This will have you feeling more confident in no time. Politicians are so confident because they say the same thing over and over and over and over and over again. You'll now be confident and stylish and by the end of the 21 days you will probably have a few new clients.

CHAPTER 9

The Gracious Realtor

"Everybody gets a car! You get a car! You get a car! And you get a car!" Who can forget than unbelievable moment on the old Oprah Winfrey show when she gave away brand new cars to every audience member? Or how on her final season, she took the entire audience on a trip to Australia? And were you also sitting at home staring in awe as she handed out free stuff on her "Favorite Things" show? There were many reasons that people loved Oprah Winfrey, and her generosity was one of them.

This chapter is all about business etiquette. If you have followed the book, your outsides are beautiful and now we just have to get your actions and insides to match. At its core, this chapter is about embracing an Oprah-like spirit of generosity, graciousness, and politeness. In this technological age where relationships break up via text message and ex-employees take to Twitter to bad-mouth you, politeness goes a long way. Good manners can help you stand out from the competition and enhance your professional reputation.

Why Manners Are Important

Has this ever happened to you: You see an up-and-coming starlet being interviewed on TV and think, "She seems really sweet." Then the next day, there is something in the news about her throwing a cell phone, passing out at a club, sexting, or leaving a drunken voicemail that is now being played on an endless loop on every entertainment media outlet. You're now thinking, "She seemed so sweet. What happened?"

You don't want people saying that about you. You want to exceed expectations. There are really three reasons why manners are important. First, you want there to be a perfect congruence between your appearance and your actions. Second, people judge you by your manners. And last but not least, good manners will help you make more friends, thereby expanding your circle of influence and referrals.

You have a polished look now, thanks to your Millionaire Real Estate Agent Makeover. You would hate to ruin that great first impression by opening your mouth and saying the wrong thing or doing something that completely obliterates any goodwill you have created. People will feel deceived and you will be thought of as untrustworthy. Imagine if you were showing a property and the outside was beautiful, landscaping was perfect, the facade of the building had been newly-painted and all the outside fixtures beautiful and perfectly matched the style of the home. Your clients would be very excited, already envisioning living in the home. Then when you take them inside the interior of the home was grimy, dingy, and looked as if squatters have been living in the home for months. It completely ruins the good feeling the potential buyers initially felt, and they are a little angry that they got excited for no reason. You don't want to be like the home with the beautiful facade with the meth lab interior.

People will judge you by your speech and your actions. If you are well-spoken, organized, and seem professional, people will invite you to events and they may even invite you to speak at events. People want to believe they will not be embarrassed by hanging out with you because you are always cursing, or you can't put together a simple sentence, or you say the most inappropriate things. Now some of this stuff is difficult for me because I like to be funny and interesting, and that is sometimes hard to do without a curse word or inappropriateness. I have to strike a balance between the two and know my audience.

Manners can help you gain more friends because people like to hear "Please" and "Thank you." They also like to receive thank you cards and congratulation notices. Just think about it—wouldn't you like to be surrounded by people that were super nice to you and were always in your corner cheering you on? Similarly, if people are not embarrassed by you, they will feel more comfortable passing along your contact information. They know you will treat their friends, family, and acquaintances appropriately. Not only that, they know that you will appreciate any referral because you call or send a card or gift to say thank you.

Even though it seems old fashioned and maybe even a little bit stuffy, manners are important. It is important to learn a little bit of etiquette, because it can have a significant impact on your business. I once had a potential employer say to someone about me, "I knew she seemed classy, and then she sent a thank you card, so I was very impressed." They didn't know that comment would make it back to me, but it helped confirm that I am giving the first impression that I want and that my actions are confirming that.

After I do styling jobs, I send out thank-you's to the people I have worked with on a photo shoot or fashion show. A thank you to a fashion show producer helped me to be called for the next fashion show. Unfortunately, that was the last time I worked with that fashion show production company because the dressers and the producers all got drunk before the fashion show so it was extremely unorganized back stage. Their lack of professionalism caused me not to want to work with them again. I do not include these jobs on my professional resume because I don't want to be associated their lack of professionalism.

Movie Characters With The Worst Manners

- Johnny Knoxville in *Bad Grandpa* - he had an "explosion" in a diner
- Meg Ryan in *When Harry Met Sally* - she had another type of "explosion" in the middle of a diner
- Luke Wilson in *Old School* - he gave the worst drunken wedding toast ever
- The 4 main characters in *The Hangover* - they showed up very late for the wedding
- Rachel McAdams in *Mean Girls* - she distributed the slam book to the entire school
- Carrie's classmates - They poured blood on her at the dance - very uncouth... and gross

A Killer (But Polite) Business App

Here's a way to market yourself as a realtor and exhibit extreme politeness that would make Emily Post proud. When a home is being put up for sale, it impacts the neighbors. A "for sale" sign or "open house" sign gets put up in front of the property. There are people coming in and out of the house at different times of the day. If there is an open house, it can impact the traffic on the street making it difficult to park, or difficult for children to play outside.

Most of the time, neighbor's don't have much of a problem with this, but they do appreciate getting a head's up. So you can go to the neighbors of the property you are representing and introduce yourself, and let them know that the property is going to be up for sale. Apologize for any inconvenience and assure them that you are going to attempt to sell the property in a timely manner to limit their inconvenience. Of course, when you go to give this little talk, you bring along some of your marketing literature and tell them they can contact your office at anytime if they need to voice any concerns.

This is something that not every realtor does, and you will definitely stand out in the marketplace. You have also just marketed yourself effectively to all of the neighbors and they will remember the courtesy you extended when they are looking for a realtor for their property.

If you want to take this killer app to the next level, you can create a custom marketing piece or letter that informs the neighbor. When you go to introduce yourself, there are going to be some households that are not going to be home at the time and you want to have something that you leave behind or mail.

I know that I have received marketing pieces in the mail from realtors about what a neighbor's property has sold for and they are trying to solicit me to sell my house and hire them as a realtor. This comes across as a little self-serving. If you position yourself as reaching out to them and giving them a little head's up, maybe giving them the hours during which you will try to schedule viewings and open houses, you will be giving them valuable information. Again, you will stand out from the crowd not only for your exceptionally professional appearance, but also for your extremely professional actions.

The Language Of Sales

As a realtor, you are a salesperson. If you have been in this field for a while, you have probably paid for and attended several sales trainings. At many of these types of trainings, they spend a lot of time talking about the language of sales and how you say things to prospects. While I am not an expert in sales, I have spent a fair amount of time learning marketing (an MBA in marketing), and I have had to learn about etiquette, so here are some phrases to help you sound a little more polite and well-mannered.

MAY I ....

The words "may I" are a more well-mannered way to ask a question. Typically, people will say "Can I" or "Could I." "May I" is a little more polite, and it's technically more grammatically correct for getting the desired answer. I remember that I had a teacher who, when students asked, "Can I," she would answer, "I don't know, can you?" When we received that response, we knew that we had asked incorrectly. I am grateful to her now for instilling that in us, but back then, Little Aisha would just roll her eyes and under her breath mutter, "Give me a break."

WOULD YOU MIND IF...

This is the phrase can replace "Can you" or "Could you". Again, it is a little more polite. Sometimes, you get a snotty response of "Yes, I would mind..." In which case proceed with caution, as this person is clearly having a bad day.

SLIGHT

This word can often soften a message. For example, to one client you might have to say, "There is a delay in receiving the closing documentation." This is not a message that a client wants to hear. You can soften this message by adding the word slight. So the new sentence would be, "There is a slight delay in receiving the closing documentation." This new phrase does not incite nearly the same amount of panic.

MIGHT

This is another word that can be used to soften or add politeness to a message. Let's take the same phrase again, "There is a delay in receiving the closing documentation." Again, this message can cause anxiety levels to rise. You can soften it by using the word might. Here is the sentence again using the word might, "There might be a delay in receiving the closing documentation." Doesn't that sound much nicer? You can further soften the message by combining slight and might. For example, "There might be a slight delay in receiving the closing documentation." That sounds like the words of a super polite and in control realtor.

I TOOK THE LIBERTY OF...

This is a great way of telling someone that you did something without their permission. It does not work in all cases. For example, you can't say, "I took the liberty of stealing your car and crashing it on the highway." There is no way that you can soften that message. However, it can help in your everyday exchanges. See how the following message sounds without this phrase.

You: I did a comparative market analysis of your home, even though we didn't discuss this in our initial phone conversation.

Client: Thanks, I appreciate that. (Client is thinking, "She is overstepping a bit.")

It doesn't sound bad, but it can come across as a little pushy. Compare that to this example using the "I took the liberty phrase;" it helps you come across as more pro-active.

You: I took the liberty of performing a comparative market analysis, even though we didn't discuss this in our initial phone conversation.

Client: Thanks! I appreciate that! (Client is thinking, "She is proactive. She'll do a great job for us.")

I'D/WE'D BE DELIGHTED

This is a great phrase to use when you are asked to do something or when you receive an invitation to an event. It sounds a lot more cultured than, "Yup." Think of how sophisticated this exchange sounds:

Colleague: Our daughter is having her 5th birthday party. We would love for you to come.

You: I'd be delighted to come! What time do you want guests to arrive?

Perhaps

Perhaps is a super polite way to disagree with someone. Imagine this exchange:

Colleague or Client: I think we should list the property for $350,000.

You: I think we should list the property for $375,000. (Client is thinking, "She is stubborn.")

Let's see how much softer and polite this exchange sounds using the word perhaps:

Colleague or Client: I think we should list the property for $350,000.

You: Perhaps we should list the property for $375,000.

See there? That sounded a lot softer and well-mannered. It also helps people to receive information better and not put up defenses. This sort of language works great in all types of relationships, not only professional ones.

Just to recap, here is a list of the polite words and expressions you should try to start sprinkling into your vocabulary:

◊ May I...
◊ Would you mind if...
◊ Slight
◊ Might
◊ I took the liberty of...
◊ I'd be/We'd be delighted
◊ Perhaps

This list is a great list to type up and print out and tape next to your computer or on your desk. You need to place it somewhere visible where it will be a constant reminder to use this language and engage in these actions.

You can visit the site www.MillionaireRealEstateAgentMakeover.com to download the list of polite words that you can tape up next to your computer.

Networking Through Graciousness

One of the great things about being a professional in the real estate industry is that there are so many opportunities for events, networking, and recognition. You turn to the real estate section of almost any newspaper and you will see how some office is honoring one of their employees. There are also many opportunities to celebrate accomplishments, such as hitting sales goals or passing exams or being recognized in the industry through one of its many trade publications. These honors are usually awarded publicly and if you are tuned in, there are many opportunities to continually award and acknowledge someone.

It also provides an excellent opportunity to join in on the bandwagon. If you see one of your colleagues or someone that you have been meaning to connect with being recognized for their achievements, you can send her a card or gift of congratulations. Of course when you send it, you will include at a minimum your business card.

This will help your name get known around the industry and you build a great reputation of being a team player. One of the things that I like to do is to have a standard card or gift that you send for this type of thing unless it is a close personal friend or family member. That way if you have an assistant, you can just say, "Could you please send the congratulations package to _____," and everyone knows what this is and exactly what to do.

The Holidays

The holidays are the time for gift giving and sending holiday greetings cards. I am a fan of sending out Happy Holidays cards because the message is applicable to any religion, agnostics, and atheists. You should have a contact database filled with past and current clients. It could get expensive sending gifts to everyone, but you should try to send a card.

Nowadays, a lot of people try to get away with sending e-cards, but it is not the same as sending a card through the mail. When it is sent through the mail, it feels like there is more effort and thought put into the gesture. My own realtor sends e-cards (she sold my house for me before I got into to doing styling for realtors). Although the gesture is appreciated, it doesn't mean as much as if she sent a beautiful card.

I like to send something personal or a little funny. I am also a fan of sending cards that look homemade. You buy these types of cards online or at stores like Target. I get so many compliments on the cards and people ask me if I made them myself. Unfortunately, I can't lie and I just tell them that I bought them like that. Sometimes I am tempted to answer, "Yes. I did make them myself. I begin constructing the cards every March."

There is a more advanced strategy you can use for client relationship management than just holiday cards. A marketing guru once told me that everyone always sends out the typical holiday cards. Why do you want to send a card when everyone else does? He actually suggests that business owners send Thanksgiving cards because you beat the rush and you really stand out with your clients. You don't end up in a pile of unopened cards.

I say, why does it have to be Thanksgiving? Why does it have to be Christmas? Really stand out and choose any holiday you want. I no longer send holiday cards to friends and family. I send Valentine's Day cards. Instead of buying a pack of cards, I handpick every card so they are all different. I say you can choose any holiday you want and go all out; it's also nice for budgeting purposes. You already have a lot of holiday expenses because of your staff. For example, you may have to pay for gifts, holiday bonuses, or holiday parties. So if you choose another holiday to celebrate with your past and present clients, you get to move some of your expenses into another month and you will really stand out because no one else is sending Earth Day cards. Your clients will start to look forward to their annual cards/gifts. For example, if you decide on Earth Day you can send it with a pack of seeds for planting a tree. If you decide on Saint Patrick's Day, you can send the card with a little green 4 leaf clover pin inside so they won't get pinched on Saint Patrick's Day. For the 4th of July, you can send the card with a little American flag. This marketing idea is only limited by your imagination.

A Client's Story

There are many milestones in a woman's life. Her first love. Marriage. Her first baby. And... her first book. Becoming an author for the first time is a big deal. So you can imagine when a first time author has a book launch party, it is a big, big deal, almost like a bride walking down the aisle. There is a lot of nervousness in the air.

This particular book launch party was planned at a nearby hotel. The décor for the party was in the colors of the book. Everyone on the team was frazzled because there was a lot to do. Are there enough books? Where is the signing table? How is the author going to enter the room? Is the food okay?

Luckily, the dress the author wore was chosen well ahead of the time, but at the last minute she realized she would be more comfortable in tights so that her legs weren't showing. I completely agreed and we got some tights that were actually very trendy and made the outfit look even more stylish (every accessory is an opportunity to either enhance or detract from the outfit). These tights took it over the top because of the pattern we chose.

The event went well. Guests were happy. The author was happy. The event planner was even starting to wind down. The event planner came over to me just as I was preparing to leave and said, "We have to do something for the team, and everyone that pitched in." Then she thrust a stack of thank you cards into my face. She said, "You write them, you are good at that. You'll make them feel special."

I took the stack of cards over to a table near the back. (Why not be full service? I shop. I style. I write cards. Need your oil changed too?) I got all the cards done, and then we needed to find out what to do for the actual venue operators. They went above and beyond; there were some last minute emergencies and they took ownership everything. The event planner came back to me and said, "We gotta really do something for them. Knock them off their feet with something special!"

Was I feeling pressure? Absolutely! Here is what I wrote: "This event has been a labor of love. Writing a book is like giving birth. Thank you for being wonderful midwives and helping to "birth" this baby. We couldn't have done it without you." Then we very quickly pulled together some other items to go along with this theme. We handed them the cards and the other items, and they were over the moon.

They asked us if we needed anything else. They wanted to work with us again. Asked us for our business cards and wanted to know how they could help give us business. It is amazing what a well-thought-out thank you can get you.

I hope by now, you realize that creating a great image is a lot more than crafting a great façade. You need to infuse it with actions, intentions, and well thought out plans. Most stylists do not go this deep, but I don't just want you to look like a different person. I want you to be a different person—a better version of yourself. I want all of your personality expressed, every quirk and every eccentricity, but I want you more confident, more polished, and making more money. To accomplish that, there is more work involved than many wardrobe stylists and image consultants are willing to do.

End-of-Chapter Bonu$:

For this end-of-chapter bonus, we are going to do it Oprah-style. You are going to add a major cornerstone to your marketing plan, your gifting policy. It is so much fun giving gifts, but instead of just leaving things to chance, we are going to develop a system of gift giving. For example, what do you do when you receive a referral, what do you do when someone signs with you, what do you do when someone closes on buying or selling a house, etc...

There are three main areas that we need to look at when considering our gifting policy:

◊ Clients

◊ Referrals

◊ Congratulatory gifts

◊ Clients

I was in a business mastermind group with a very accomplished and successful realtor who lived and worked in the Maui area. As you can imagine, this is a very affluent area with top-notch clientele. I mean, Oprah has a house there (I know it is sounding like I want to "single white female" Oprah Winfrey, but I just really admire her and she is going to appear in this chapter a lot. I promise to tone down my Oprah obsession in subsequent chapters.) When her clients closed on her property, her gift would be a very expensive piece of art. In the realtor relationship, you get to know your clients and their taste well. This piece of art, while it was a fantastic gift, was also a great marketing piece.

Whenever the clients had visitors at the house and someone asked about the piece of art, the person would say that their realtor gave it to them. What a great way to stand out and market yourself! I thought the idea was pure genius.

So, while you may not have tens of thousands of dollars to spend on a gift, you can probably spring for a nice gift that will leave people talking. Try to leave your mark so that your gift will do the marketing for you.

The other thing that I want to emphasize is that presentation is everything. It helps build anticipation and makes the receiver of the gift even more excited about receiving the gift. Can you put the gift in a gift bag, wrap it, or just wrap a bow around it?

Unless you are dealing with extremely high net worth individuals, the gift does not have to extremely customized as when you have to rack your brain to come up with a unique gift for people that already have everything. I recommend that you come up with 3 to 5 great client gifts.

For example, the gift could be a bottle of champagne and a set of nice champagne glasses so that the clients can toast the close of the transaction. You can always customize this. For example, for the couple that talked about how they loved their honeymoon in France, you can make sure to get a bottle of French champagne. (Please, don't send nasty emails. I am well aware that many people think there is only French champagne and everything else is sparkling wine).

Or you can deliver a Home Depot gift card inside of an envelope tied with a bunch of orange balloons. The idea is to be creative and be over the top if you can, because it gets people talking. If your budget isn't that big, that just means you have to make up for it with creativity and originality.

You want to come up with 3 to 5 ideas, because you want this process to be turnkey so you'll know exactly where to go, what to buy, and how to put the gift together. Also, if you are going to be a Millionaire Real Estate Agent, you will eventually need to have a staff. And when you have a client that closes, you want to be able to say, "Send gift #5," or "Send the home depot gift." Your staff member will then know the amount the gift card should be and how to prepare the gift. All you have to do is sit back and wait for the thank you call and practice saying, "You're welcome."

Referrals

While great client closing gifts can help you get referrals, you also want to have a stand out gift for referrals. I recommend a two-tier approach:

◊   A standard gift or card for a standard referral

◊   A gift or card for when a referral closes

The standard referral is just for any referral you receive, whether it goes anywhere or not. The reason why is that someone took time out of their day to pass along your name and contact information. You want to acknowledge that action and encourage more of it. So just reaching out with a card or gift helps acknowledge the referral and encourages the person do more of that type of action. Because all of these referrals do not result in an actual commission, you may not want to spend big bucks in this area, but you definitely need to come up with a policy for it. Whether you send a card and an email, or you make a phone call and send a gift card. It is really up to you, how you want to acknowledge the action. I would recommend making this into a system as well, meaning at the end of the week you see all the referrals that came in and you make your thank you calls and/or send out all of your cards.

The gift for when a referral closes is a little bit different. This referral actually resulted in money in your pocket, so you can spend a little more for this. I used to have a bouquet of flowers delivered for this and I would usually have it delivered to their place of work so that when people ask where the flowers came from, my name would be mentioned and potentially result in additional referrals. Flower delivery makes everyone feel special and it can be relatively inexpensive now due to all the online websites that regularly offers specials.

Congratulatory gifts

This last gift category of your gifting policy was already discussed earlier in the chapter. This consists of little gifts or cards that you send out to your colleagues and other industry professionals.

A lot of this might seem excessive. You might ask other real estate professionals if they do any of these things and the response will usually be, "No, I don't do any of that." But just ask yourself—do you want to be like them, or do you want to become a Millionaire Real Estate Agent? If you're reaching for the top, you have to start thinking and acting differently from your colleagues.

CHAPTER 10

The Millionaire Realtor

The subtitle of this book is, "Is your sense of style limiting your paycheck?" The answer is that research seems to suggest that this is the case. There is already plenty of research on how looks can impact a person's career, but nothing specific to the real estate field. So I did my own research. Even though many people may expect me to be some flaky wardrobe stylist, I actually have my MBA and was a graduate assistant for two economic professors. Analyzing data and performing research do not scare me (see you can be stylish and brainy).

The result of this research was published under the title, "How the Rich Get Richer: What your real estate headshot secretly says about your income bracket." Now I had real data and real results to give people when they asked why I placed so much importance on appearance.

In the rest of the book, when we were trying to determine your color season or body shape, you compared yourselves to celebrities. But in reality, none of you reading this book wants to be an actress or a pop singer. You want to be a successful real estate agent that is very successful and making lots of money.

In this chapter, we are going to compare you to the most successful female realtors in the country. I looked at the Top 250 realtors in the country by sales volume, and then only looked at the subsection of female realtors. And then I did what any self-respecting wardrobe stylist would do—I evaluated their professional headshots that were used in their marketing materials. I recorded colors, accessories, patterns, suits, jackets, and other interesting details, trying to see how these uber-successful realtors dressed. I was trying to unlock the formula to see what I could implement with my clients so that their professional head shots screamed success.

But I was missing a piece. I needed to compare these super-talented Top 250 realtors to a random sample of regular realtors (people not on the Top 250 list for 2013). If the successful realtors did something different from the less successful realtors, then I had it. That would be the difference; that would be the key to realtor success. Did I discover any differences? You bet I did, but we will get into that in a minute.

Now at this point, some of you might be thinking, "Well, that is not really fair. Obviously, if a realtor works in Beverly Hills you can't compare her to a realtor in rural Kansas. Of course there will be differences." And you are absolutely right, so that is why I made the two groups match geographically. For example, on my successful realtor list I had five realtors from Beverly Hills, so I compared them to five other randomly selected realtors from Beverly Hills. Even in wealthy areas, you are going to have more elite realtors; there are plenty of realtors in Beverly Hills that did not make the Top 250 list. I want to know what the Top 250 are doing because those are the best practices that I want to implement. To give you an idea of the chunk of change these realtors are generating, one of the realtors in Beverly Hills had a sales volume of over $338 million, and she wasn't even the heaviest hitter on the list.

The next thing that comes to people's mind is, "Of course, they dress nice. They have the money to dress nice." This brings us to the chicken and the egg problem—what happens first? Do you dress better first so that you get better clients and make more money to dress even nicer? Or do you first need to get better clients and then that enables you to dress better? This circular argument can be ended with one simple question: If dressing nice wasn't important, why after people start making more money do they dress nicer?

We have all seen this arc as well with actresses or singers. Just starting out, they are better than average looking...but after several years, they are stunningly gorgeous and look more polished and put together. Why would they go through all that trouble?

Maybe you have to be what you want. You want more money, you want better clients? Then you have to step up and be better! You attract what you are.

This point was proven perfectly in Barbara Corcoran's book, "If You Don't Have Big Breasts, Then Put Ribbons in Your Pigtails." Barbara Corcoran is the mogul of real estate. She sold her real estate empire for $66 million (she started with an initial investment of $1,000). You can watch her hold her own once a week on the hit TV show Shark Tank. She also has some great advice for realtors and business owners in her books, TV show, and public speeches.

In her book, Chapter 2 is dedicated entirely to the topic of dressing better. The title of the chapter is "Paint the Rocks White and the Whole Yard Will Look Lovely." She explains with her first real estate commission check she went to the legendary department store Bergdorf Goodman and bought a luxurious coat. She talks about how she now felt like she looked the part and she felt more confident. She goes on to explain in the summary lesson at the end of the chapter that people really do judge a book by its cover.

She says, "By dressing the part of someone successful. I was forced to measure up to my new image." She goes on to conclude, "... perception creates reality. Most people think it is the other way around." So there you have it from a very successful female real estate mogul. She provides an answer to the chicken and the egg question. You must first create the perception of success, and then it becomes a reality.

Why Do The Rich Get Richer?

Back to my own research and the key takeaways from weeks and weeks of research. You want to know what is different about the women that made it on to the Top 250 realtors list, so let's dive in.

TAKEAWAY #1 - THESE LADIES CARE ABOUT MARKETING

As you can imagine, this research was very tedious. It was very time-consuming to research all of these realtors and find their professional headshots, because I started out researching the women that were in the Top 250, and then later researched the random sample of realtors.

After researching the 10th realtor from the less successful realtor group, I realized that it was taking me much longer to track down these women. The realtors from the successful group made sure they had a significant online presence. They had websites, online profiles, social media, etc... It was easy for me to find them, which means it was easy for potential clients to find them. I used a basic google search to track down these women; this is the same way that potential clients could find them.

In addition, the photos of the more successful realtors were more prominent. They made their marketing message personal. Their photos were on the home pages of their websites; I didn't have to hunt around to find them. Along with their photos, there were complete professional profiles of them.

Their overall marketing message was also more coordinated. The headshot photos matched the style of the websites and other marketing pieces. Overall, they created a great presentation that tells potential clients that they are detail-oriented, organized, and have their act together.

With the less successful realtors, the absence of a web presence increased by 62.5%. Seems to me, the number one way to start standing out from the crowd is to craft a significant web presence, because there are so few realtors that do. The successful realtor group seemed to understand this and made sure that piece of their marketing plan was thoroughly in place.

This concept was covered at a high level in the chapter on color. You create a color palette for yourself and then make all of your marketing materials reflect that color palette. This will help you to have a more coordinated marketing message and start looking like the Millionaire Real Estate Agent you will become.

Takeaway #2 - These ladies care about professionalism

Initially, this may seem to be the same thing as takeaway #1, but I promise you it is different. For example, as a realtor, I could have a significant online marketing presence. I could have a website, a blog, and social media sites, but they could all be mismatched. I could have a headshot that I took with my webcam. I could have pictures of me at a bachelorette party where I was so wasted that people mistake the photo for Nick Nolte's mug shot. I know this is an extreme example, but it helps explain how the two takeaways are different.

The successful realtor group showed more professionalism in two ways: their attire and their online presence. For example, more realtors from the successful group wore jackets in their headshots. This shows that using their attire to convey a professional image was more important to the elite group of realtors.

As a fashion professional, I do not think a suit with a jacket is always necessary to convey a professional image. However, when you think you need to be dressed up and professional, the first thing that comes to mind is a suit. The fact that they wore more suit jackets shows that they performed this thought process more.

Attire was not the only way the more successful realtors conveyed professionalism. For example, one of the successful realtors from Malibu wore jeans and a t-shirt in her photo to help convey the beach lifestyle which most of her clients are looking for. However, the photo was professionally taken and staged on the beach. Her business partner was posed next also in jeans and a t-shirt. The rest of her website was extremely professional almost in an attempt to offset the casualness of her photo.

Takeaway #3 - These ladies care about details

Oprah Winfrey threw an event never to be repeated—her Legends Ball. This initial event turned into a whole weekend extravaganza. This weekend was so magical that it was caught on film and aired as a primetime special. In watching the preparation for the weekend, Oprah said a phrase that will stay with me forever, "Love is in the details."

No detail was overlooked for this event. The invitations, the centerpieces, the decorations, the gifts were all stunning. Anybody attending this event would think, "Somebody spent a lot of time, energy, and money, thinking about this. We must be very important to them." All you had to do was look at the invitation and you would know that there was so much detail involved in this, that there is loved infused into it, much like an artist infuses love into every sculpture or painting. Love really is in the details.

The elite group of realtors embodied this. In their headshots, the outfits were better, there was a greater range of colors, more accessories, and just more interesting elements such as colorful scarves or an interesting print pattern. There was a greater attention to detail, and people are drawn to that. It is like being at a museum and looking at an intricate painting of a woman where it looks every strand of hair was meticulously painted into place. You would be drawn to the painting.

I think the attention to detail conveys a lot more if you are a realtor. I believe that it also indicates that you will pay attention to details for your clients. There are so many things to deal with when you are buying or selling a house. A potential client wants to believe you won't let anything slip through the cracks. I think the detail orientation in your appearance and how your business is presented helps to sub-consciously communicate that message.

The Fab Five

The "fab five" are the five specific things that the Top 250 did differently from the random sample of realtors.

ONLINE MARKETING

The Top 250 were much better at online marketing. They were much better at creating a web presence and web persona which made it easier for researchers to track down professional photos. The absence of a significant web presence increased by 62.5% with the random sample of female real estate professionals. There are many ways to make your appearance and your professional head shot a profitable part of your marketing plan.

COLORS

There were differences in the colors worn in the professional real estate photos of The Top 250—they wore a greater range of colors. Their variety of colors increased by 36%, with colors ranging from the traditional black to the hot pink. Even with this greater variety, there were more women in the Top 250 who opted to where all black in their photos, 27% (Top 250) versus 15% (random sample). In executing this research, one was able to mimic a consumer shopping for a realtor by having to go through numerous websites and photos. Color was the single most important thing that made a realtor stand out, and there were several colors that came across as refreshing after wading through hundreds of websites.

Here are the top 10 color choices:

Top 250 Realtors	Random Sample
Black	Black
Black and Ivory	Black and Ivory
Ivory	Ivory
Blue	Red
Red	Light Blue
Black and Blue	Pink
Black and Tan	Black and Light Blue
Green	Black and Red
Ivory and Blue	Gray
Ivory and Navy	Black and Light Pink

As you can see from both columns, there was a lot of black. Black did look sleek and professional. When all else fails, wear black; however, as I mentioned earlier, after wading through hundreds of real estate head shots, the ones that made you pause and pay attention where the ones that were not wearing black. So if you want to stand out from the competition, I would actually recommend something other than black.

You'll notice something else by looking at the list above. The Top 250 list incorporates a lot more bold colors, such as blue, green, navy. The random sample of less successful realtors uses softer colors such as light blue, light pink, and gray. While there is a place in branding for soft colors, bold colors are what grab attention. Clearly, the women in Top 250 realtors understand this. They want the attention and they want the clients.

Accessories

The Top 250 realtors accessorized better in their professional photos. For instance, 64% of the Top 250 wore earrings in their photos versus only 35% for the random sample of female real estate professionals. There were also more instances of scarves, brooches, or other accessories worn by the Top 250 professionals. However, there was one accessory that was worn equally as often, a necklace. In both groups of professionals, approximately 40% of them wore necklaces in their professional photos.

So although it appears that both groups of realtors enjoy wearing necklaces in their headshots, the Top 250 know how to fully accessorize. What I found interesting is that more women in the random sample wore necklaces than earrings. The headshot is all about your face, and earrings can be a great additional way to beautifully frame your face.

Outerwear

The Top 250 put on a more professional appearance by wearing a jacket or blazer in their photos. 56% of the Top 250 wore a jacket in their professional photos versus 47% of the random sample. If you are not comfortable wearing a jacket, there are many ways to look professional without a jacket. One of the Top 250 realtors wore a great dress without a jacket for her headshot and the photo looked like she could have been on the cover of Forbes magazine.

Details

The Top 250 made their photos more interesting by including interesting elements in their photos to help them stand out. 46% of the Top 250 realtors included interesting details in their outfits versus only 33% of the random sample of realtors. These interesting details included everything from silk fabrics to busy prints and layered necklaces to brooches. There is a thin line between pleasantly interesting and messy. Many of the realtors who were aiming for an interesting look ended up looking more like a jumbled mess. These often-repeated wardrobe mistakes are easy to avoid if you follow a few simple rules.

Men vs Women

Now you know how you stack up against realtors on the Top 250 realtors in the country. But do you know that as a woman, you also on average do not measure up to the men in your industry?

According to the Bureau of Labor Statistics, in 2012 the average male real estate agent/broker made $1,031 a week, while the average female real estate agent/broker makes $680 a week. You are earning about 66% of your male counterpart's earnings. To correct this imbalance, you need to use every tool in your arsenal to get better clients, better listings, and more referrals. The Millionaire Real Estate Agent Makeover is a great way to make that happen; implementing the business ideas can propel you ahead of your male colleagues.

This earnings gap exists even though women outnumber men in the real estate field. There are 195,000 female real estate brokers/agents and only 134,000 male real estate brokers/agents.

Millionaire Real Estate Agent Style Profile: Barbra Corcoran

Barbara Corcoran is the author of best-selling books and the only female "shark" investor on the TV show Shark Tank. She earned her spot by borrowing $1,000 to start her own real estate company, The Corcoran Group, and growing the company to sell it for $66 million dollars in 2001. If you look at her magazine cover for Entrepreneur magazine, it has Millionaire Real Estate Agent style appeal (you can google the image). Instead of wearing very conservative black, she is in a bright yellow (but professional) dress, small but tasteful dangling earrings, a multi-strand necklace, and a simple gold bracelet. The outfit stands out, is still professional, yet feminine.

Style Grade: A+

Millionaire Real Estate Agent Style Profile: Katrina Campins

Katrina Campins rose to fame on season 1 of the Donald Trump produced TV show "The Apprentice." She then appeared on Bravo's TV show "Miami Social" that follows around several friends that live and worked in South Beach, Florida. She is the real estate agent to many celebrities and athletes. She also had her very own short lived TV show on The Style Network, "Hot Listings Miami." In the photo featured in the OK Magazine article "12 Reasons Katrina Campins, Star of Hot Listings Miami, is My New Girl Crush, Role Model and Best Friend At The Same Time" (google it). She is keeping her outfit trendy and professional, with a hint of femme fatale. The color combination is killer with a blue dress and green blazer. She accessorizes with a long gold necklace and a green oversized ring. The makeup adds additional color with red lips and red nail polish. While this look might not work for everyone and might not work for all ages, the foundation of the outfit is great. Keep the great color combo; switch out for a dress that is better for your body type. This outfit definitely says, "Pay attention to me," and it has some serious Millionaire Real Estate Agent style appeal.

Style Grade: A

Millionaire Real Estate Agent Style Profile: Valerie Fitzgerald

Valerie Fitzgerald and her team have their own show on HGTV called "Selling LA." If you visit the home page of her website, www.

valeriefitzgerald.com, you'll see that she has a great headshot. She has a picture of herself in a white blouse, but the blouse has ruffles down the front and an interesting print. You can also clearly see that she is wearing a white necklace and small dangling earrings. The look is a little more laid back than professional, but maybe fits in a little better with the relaxed southern California look. Her outfit is definitely more laid back. I would have loved to see a little bit more color, but she somewhat made up for it with the interesting details in her blouse.

Style Grade: B

WTF

I was watching TV recently. Okay, okay, I was watching one of the Real Housewives episodes. (I swear I watch PBS too!) One of the housewives was moving to a very affluent area and her realtor stopped by just to check in and see how she liked the house. I was surprised by the realtor's appearance. Here was this woman selling very nice homes in an affluent area and she was on a national TV show, and she looked like she was on her way to the market. It was a huge opportunity wasted.

I believe the realtor may have been a friend of the family. Here the spotlight was on her and she had a chance to appear professional and poised, and she wasted it. After I stopped screaming at the screen, I thought, "How many of us waste opportunities every day?"

- ◊ The man in line behind us at the coffee shop may make the perfect next boyfriend.
- ◊ The woman next to you at the beauty salon may make the perfect business partner.
- ◊ The lady with you waiting at the doctor's office is buying a home next month.

- ◊ The old woman ahead of you at the dry cleaners belongs to every social club in town and the referrals you receive from her can put your kids through college.
- ◊ The friend of a friend would love your advice on selling her home, but you have been too un-confident to approach her.

We all waste tons of opportunities every day by not putting our best face forward.

That realtor could have leveraged that opportunity and catapulted herself to millionaire status. If she was already there, she could have achieved multimillionaire celebrity real estate agent status.

I don't want that to be you. I want you catching every opportunity with a big gigantic butterfly net. If you want to catch opportunities, you need the right bait... you need the right outfits... and you need this book.

Best of luck with your Millionaire Real Estate Agent Makeover, and if you ever have the opportunity for a national spotlight, give me call and I'll give you the perfect outfit. I don't want you to be the cautionary tale for when this book prints its second edition.

End-Of-Chapter Bonu$:

We are at the end of the book and your Millionaire Real Estate Agent makeover is almost complete. You have looked at all the steps required to get to that level and you have learned from my research, what the millionaire real estate agents are doing and what they look like. I think you now have a really good sense of what a millionaire real estate agent truly is.

So let's imagine her:

What is her health like? What does her body look like?

What do her relationships look like? Does she have a spouse, life partner? Does she have kids? Is it a happy household? What is her relationship like with friends and coworkers?

What does her financial life look like? How much does she make a month? What is her bank account balance? Does she have investments?

How does the millionaire real estate agent dress? Use the space below to record your answer:

What does her business look like? How are things run? What does her office/home office look like?

What does she do for fun?

Have you filled out all of the sections above? If not, go back and write this information down before you proceed.

All of your answers to the questions above are your to-do list. This is your list of goals. You have identified above what you want your life to look like, so get started!

Here are some ideas to help you get started:

◊ Transform your answers above into a list of goals and tape it someplace where you will see it every day.

◊ Write your answers down on 3x5 index cards and review them every morning and evening to help you remember your goals.

◊ Take your answers and transform them into a vision board. Post your vision board where you will see it often.

You can make this millionaire real estate agent lifestyle your reality. This book is just one step in the process. It's a very stylish step in stiletto heels. After all, the journey of a thousand miles begins with a single step.... into a more stylish version of you.

Journey well!

Appendix A:

101 Accessories List

Anklet
Arm Band
Arm Bracelet
Aviator Sunglasses
Backpack
Bangle Bracelets
Baseball Cap
Beanie
Belt
Beret
Bolo Tie
Bow Tie
Brooch
Carry-On Luggage
Chandelier Earrings
Charm Bracelet
Choker
Cigarette Case
Clutch
Cocktail Ring
Coin Purse

Collar Necklace
Compact Mirror
Cosmetic Bag
Cross-body Bag
Cuff Bracelet
Diamond Stud Earrings
Dog Tags (military inspired necklace)
Drop Earrings
Earbuds
Envelope Clutch
Exotic Skin Handbag
Eyeglasses
Fanny Pack
Faux Ffur Sscarf
Fishnet Sstockings
Garment Bag
Gentleman's Hat
Hair Rribbon
Handkerchief
Headband
Hobo Bag
Hoop Earrings
Investment Handbag
iPod
Jeweled Barrette
Jewelry Pouch
Keychain
Keyring
Knee- high Stockings
Lace Tights
Laptop Bag
Leather Bracelet
Leather Gloves
Leather Handbag
Locket Necklace
Luggage

Men's Watch
Metallic Clutch
Muff
Multi-finger Rings
Nail Polish
Oversized Belt Buckle
Pattern Stockings
Pearl Necklace
Perfume
Pocket Watch
Ponytail Holder
Rosary or Prayer Beads
Sarongs
Scarf
Shawl
Signet Ring
Silk Scarf
Simple Chain
Smart Phone
Socks
Spanx
Statement Necklace
Stationery
Stockings
Straw Tote
Sunglasses
Sunhat
Suspenders
Sweater Tights
Tablet
Tablet Case
Tattoo (fake or real)
Thin Belt
Tie
Tie Clip
Tie Pin

Toe Ring
Tote Bag
Umbrella
Wallet
Watch
Wayfarers
Wide Belt
Wow Earrings

Appendix B:

7 Deadly Sins of a Head Shot Photo

◊ Thou shall not use spray tanner the day before a photo shoot. Allow plenty of time before your big day for tanning mishaps.

◊ Thou shall not try a new hairstyle or color right before the photo shoot. Get your hair trimmed and your color retouched a day or two in advance, in case of mishaps that need to be beautified.

◊ Thou shall not stay out all night the night before your photo shoot. Unless you think bloodshot eyes say, "Let me sell your house," get a decent night's sleep. You spent all this money to have great photos; don't see this investment go down the drain.

◊ Thou shall not get a facial right before the photo shoot. Get it one to two days before your photo shoot. Facials can cause irritation and bring up all the guck under the surface of your skin and cause breakouts. Now is not the time to try something new. Unless you want to find a photographer that photographs outer space, because they will know how to take pictures of craters.

◊ Thou shall not diet to exhaustion right before your photo shoot. Two days of starvation will not get you six-pack abs and a size 0 waist. You'll just look miserable in your photo, like you would kill a man for a single McDonald's French fry. Also, photographers don't like it if you faint on set.

◊ Thou shall not be diva on set. Yes you should voice your opinions and communicate your vision, but don't request to have only blue M&M's or Evian water available on set. You would be surprised by the number of people that flip the diva switch on set. Remember, you want these people to become part of your network, so act like a professional and check your diva-tude at the door.

◊ Thou shall not be disorganized. Be respectful of people's time and space. If you are organized, you will be able to easily transition into your different looks and you might even have fun. If you are unorganized, you are frantic and it may come out in the photos. Make sure your outfits and accessories are organized ahead of time and save yourself and others a lot of headaches.

Appendix C:

Answers to Chapter 4's Fill-in the Blanks

Here are the fill in the blank answers to the questions in Chapter 5 - The Gilded Realtor:

- ◊ 64% of the Top 250 Realtors wore earrings versus only 35% of a random sample of realtors.
- ◊ 56% of the top 250 Realtors wore a jacket versus only 47% of the random sample of realtors

Appendix D:

Your Color Season

- ◊ Group A = Spring
- ◊ Group B = Summer
- ◊ Group C = Autumn
- ◊ Group D = Winter

Appendix E:

Emergency Checklist

Here is the full list of emergency checklist items:

- ◊ Basic sewing kit
- ◊ Bobby pins
- ◊ Extra business cards
- ◊ Lint brush
- ◊ Lip balm
- ◊ Lotion
- ◊ Mints
- ◊ Ponytail holders/rubber bands
- ◊ Quick dry clear nail polish
- ◊ Safety pins
- ◊ Stain remover pen
- ◊ Sunscreen
- ◊ Tampons/Maxi pads
- ◊ Travel nail kit
- ◊ Tweezers
- ◊ Wrinkle releaser spray

Appendix F:

Style Net Worth Quiz

How many suits do you own?
- A. 1... the loneliest number
- B. 1/2... I have bottoms and jackets, but they don't necessarily go together
- C. 2 or more... my policy is "The more the merrier"
- D. 0... I prefer not to be weighed down by such things

When is the last time you wore a color other than black, gray, or brown (pajamas don't count)?
- A. I think about wearing color, but black is slimming and my thighs are addicted to black
- B. Today... I try to wear as many colors as possible at any given time (you're like a walking beach ball)
- C. I am wearing some color right now while reading this book
- D. Well, since pajamas don't count, then I may need hypnosis to think that far back

Do you have a tailor?
  A. No, it looks just fine off the rack
  B. Yes, my tailor modified my Elvira Halloween costume so I can wear it year-round to the office
  C. Yes, almost all of my structured professional clothing has been altered
  D. No... by tailor, do you mean Taylor Swift?

When someone looks at your real estate photo, what do they think?
  A. This must be her DMV photo
  B. Wow, she's a Hot Tamale
  C. Nice pic; attractive and professional
  D. That is why you shouldn't drink and drive; your mug shot may end up on the internet

At an open house, do attendees:
  A. Hand you their drink glasses
  B. Think they have walked into a nightclub when they see your outfit
  C. Come up and ask you about the property because they know you are in charge
  D. Go right past you as if you blend into the background

If someone walked into your office, they would think:
  A. I should ask her who is in charge
  B. This person had a rough day on the job
  C. This person is the boss
  D. Why is the cleaning lady here during the day?

Your nails can be described as:
- A. not glamorous, but clean and trimmed down with no polish
- B. polished and extra trendy; the ring finger has a leopard print, the pinky has a rhinestone, and the thumb has your boyfriend's initials
- C. trimmed, polished, and shiny
- D. the love child of a bag lady and a feral cat

Your makeup routine can be described as
- A. Chapstick most days and lip gloss on the really good days like my birthday or having lunch with the Duchess of York
- B. Drag queen-esque
- C. Polished and professional
- D. Cold water and a towel... on a good day

In the movie about your life, the character that plays you would be most similar to
- A. Annette Bening in American Beauty (her character is a realtor)
- B. Julia Roberts in Erin Brockovich - (you may even have that same bustier hanging in your closet)
- C. Meryl Streep in The Devil Wears Prada (minus the condescending glare)
- D. Sandra Bullock in Miss Congeniality (pre-makeover)

Your confidence about your career can be described as
- A. A solid C+
- B. Borderline bi-polar (high one minute and low the next minute)
- C. Skyrockets in flight
- D. Keeping an eye on the help wanted ads

If You Answered Mostly A's:

You're on the road to style wealth.

You already have great style habits, in my estimation. You just need a little more polish to really start shining. Fill in your wardrobe with the few missing pieces from Chapter 1. Pay special attention to Chapter 4, because this will add some serious power and elegance to what you are already doing.

If You Answered Mostly B's:

Paycheck to paycheck...

Your style bank account is full some days and running a negative balance on other days. No one would ever call you boring, but there are ways to build some more consistency into your sense of style that can help you to start building up some style equity. Build the basics into your wardrobe as found in chapter 1; this will help you enormously in that area. So what are you waiting for...get to reading!

If You Answered Mostly C's:

Quite a nest egg!

That's quite a nest egg you have there. You may have hit millionaire real estate agent status by the time you finish this paragraph. You have most of this down, but this book should be a great refresher course for you. Fill in the few gaps there may be in managing your appearance and first impressions. Make sure to implement the end-of-chapter bonu$es so that you can leverage all the hard work you have already put in. Keep up the good work!

If You Answered Mostly D's:

Destitute...

If there were fashion welfare, you would be on it. You need some assistance. Don't consider it a handout, consider it a hand up. You need to start at Chapter 1 and don't come up for air until you hit chapter 5. Don't get discouraged! If I learned anything from movies, it's that a makeover works on the most hopeless cases. You'll even get to have a great montage scene of you trying on clothes while pop music plays over the scene. I believe in you. You can do it! Just take a deep breath and dive in.

Appendix G:

The "Just One Thing" Plan

This is the plan of action for the busy women out there. This is a plan for the skeptics; for the women that would rather dip their toe in the water rather than take the plunge. Here is the plan, where if you can just implement one thing from every chapter to move your style (and hopefully your income) forward.

Chapter 1

There are the 12 Apostles of Style, but if I had to choose just one item for you to get, it would be this. Buy a stylish trench coat. A trench coat is a great buy because you can put it on over anything and look more stylish and put together. If you had to get only one item on the checklist, it would be this.

____ Buy a stylish trench coat

Chapter 2

There are four items under NEFT-Y for grooming. If I had to only choose one for you to do, it would be to get your eyebrows groomed on a regular bases (unless you have a serious problem with facial hair in which case, skip eyebrows and proceed directly to facial hair).

____ Groom eyebrows regularly

Chapter 3

How to choose... so may options in this chapter. I'll choose something that will make you want to do more: get one item professionally tailored to accentuate your body's positives.

____ Get one item tailored to your body

Chapter 4

This is tough. Chapter 3 is essentially an entire exercise on how to brand yourself with color. Instead of creating an entire color palette, your one thing is to go through the exercise and choose one color.

____ Choose one personal color

Chapter 5

How can you choose just one accessory? It is the fashion equivalent of Sophie's Choice. But if you were to put a gun to my head, I would choose the investment handbag. This makes a huge statement and can make jeans and a t-shirt look chic and stylish.

____ Buy an investment handbag

Chapter 6

This one is easy. Chapter 4 is all about the power outfit. There is only one item on this checklist.

____ Buy a power outfit and have it fitted

Chapter 7

This is another easy one. Get new headshots. Done... Next...

____ Get new headshots

Chapter 8

There are so many confidence-building exercises in this chapter, but here is the one that will make you feel the best and spread some good cheer: Compliments, compliments, compliments! Give them generously, and practice receiving them with grace and confidence.

____ Play the Compliments Game

Chapter 9

I really, really, really want you to do all of these things, but if I must choose one:

____ Develop a gift policy for clients - be creative!

Chapter 10

The idea of this chapter is to learn what we can from Millionaire Real Estate Agents. 64% of them wore earrings in their head shots. Guess what your one thing is?

____ Wear earrings every day

About Aisha

Aisha Jones' MBA could also stand for Maniacally Buying Apparel. She is a b-school corporate climber turned fashion expert that is part fashionista and part mad scientist in a stylish leopard print lab coat with her patent pending invention, Style Recipe Cards, that guarantees 20 compliments in 20 days.

She has worked as a wardrobe artist on music videos, photo shoots, fashion shows, and pageant styling. If you asked her what her one wish would be, her answer would be a dressing room mirror that erases cellulite followed by world peace. (In case anyone from the U.N. is reading this, she wants them to know that world peace is a close second, practically a photo finish.)

She is trying to make the world more stylish one outfit at a time. She, and offers a free makeover at www.NoMorePlainJane.com and her just for realtors makeover www.MillionaireRealEstateAgentMakeover.com

Resources

Style Recipe Cards

My greatest achievement to date. This is auto-pilot. It allows women to stop worrying about what to wear and just learn how to count their compliments. Each collection consists of 10 cards for outfits. You are given shopping lists and ways to mix 'n' match outfits like a true pro. Visit www.StyleRecipeCards.com for more information.

Free Makeover

In all honestly, more information is contained in the makeover in this book, than in what is provided in the No More Plain Jane Makeover. However, fill free to check it out, visit www.NoMorePlainJane.com to learn more.

Blog/Website

www.AishaJones.com is the headquarters for all of the style and makeover information. You can get access to products, services, or just free information and offers.

Newsletter

The newsletter subscribers are the first ones to have access to how-to style videos. The have special access to discounts, products, and are the only ones with access to the Style Recipe Cards boutique.

To subscribe to the newsletter you can either complete the No More Plain Jane Makeover at www.NoMorePlainJane.com

YouTube

My YouTube channel is filled with many how-to videos to help you mix and match and create a wardrobe worthy of your dreams for yourself. These are very short videos that provide easy to do information. Visit www.AishaJones.com for links to my YouTube channel.

Social Media

You can also connect with me though various social media channels. Makeover and wardrobe advice are given out liberally. It is a great way to stay motivated through the makeover process. Visit www.AishaJones.com for links to my YouTube channel.

Aisha Jones

www.ingramcontent.com/pod-product-compliance
Lightning Source LLC
Chambersburg PA
CBHW051647170526
45167CB00001B/366